DAUGHTERS
OF THE PURITANS

THE HOME OF LYDIA MARIA CHILD
AT WAYLAND, MASSACHUSETTS

DAUGHTERS
OF THE PURITANS

A Group of Brief Biographies

BY

SETH CURTIS BEACH

Essay Index Reprint Series

BOOKS FOR LIBRARIES PRESS, INC.

FREEPORT, NEW YORK

First published 1905
Reprinted 1967

CONTENTS

I
CATHARINE MARIA SEDGWICK

CATHARINE MARIA SEDGWICK

During the first half of the nineteenth century, Miss Sedgwick would doubtless have been considered the queen of American letters, but, in the opinion of her friends, the beauty of her character surpassed the merit of her books. In 1871, Miss Mary E. Dewey, her life-long neighbor, edited a volume of Miss Sedgwick's letters, mostly to members of her family, in compliance with the desire of those who knew and loved her, " that some printed memorial should exist of a life so beautiful and delightful in itself, and so beneficent in its influence upon others." Truly a " life beautiful in itself and beneficent in its influence," the reader will say, as he lays down this tender volume.

Catharine Maria Sedgwick was born at Stockbridge, Mass., in 1789, the first year of the presidency of George Washington. She was a descendant from Robert Sedgwick, major-general under Cromwell, and governor of Jamaica. Her father, Theodore Sedgwick, was a country boy, born in 1746, upon a barren farm in one of the hill-towns of Connecticut. Here the family opened a country store, then added a tavern, and with the combined industries of farm, store and tavern, Theodore, most fortunate of the sons if not the favorite, was sent to Yale college, where he remained, until, in the last year of his course, he managed to get himself expelled. He began the study of theology, his daughter suggests, in a moment of contrition over expulsion from college, but soon turned to the law for which he had singular aptitude. He could not have gone far in his legal career when, before the age of twenty-one, he married a beautiful girl whose memory he always tenderly cherished, as well he might considering his part in the tragedy of her early death. He had taken small pox, had been duly quarantined and discharged but his young wife combed out the tangles of his matted hair, caught the disease, and died, within a year after marriage.

Marriage was necessary in those days, his daughter suggests, and the year of conventional widowhood having expired, Mr. Sedgwick, then at the age of twenty-three, married Miss Pamela Dwight, the mother of his four sons, all successful lawyers, and his three daughters, all exemplary women. The second Mrs. Sedgwick

CATHARINE MARIA SEDGWICK

was presumably more beautiful than the first; certainly she was more celebrated. She is immortalized by her portrait in Griswold's " American Court," and by a few complimentary lines in Mrs. Ellet's " Queens of American Society."

Theodore Sedgwick rose to distinction by his energies and talents but, as we have seen, he was of sufficiently humble origin, which could not have been greatly redeemed by expulsion from college; while at the age of twenty-three, that must have been his chief exploit. Social lines were very firmly drawn in that old colonial society, before the plough of the Revolution went through it, and there was no more aristocratic family than the Dwights, in Western Massachusetts.

Madame Quincy gives an account of a visit, in her girlhood, paid to the mother of Miss Pamela, Madame Dwight, in her " mansion-house," and says that her husband, Brig.-Gen. Joseph Dwight, was " one of the leading men of Massachusetts in his day." Madame Dwight was presumably not inferior to her husband. She was daughter of Col. Williams, of Williamstown, who commanded a brigade in the old French War, and whose son founded Williams College. A daughter of Madame Dwight,

[3]

older than Pamela, married Mark Hopkins, " a distinguished lawyer of his time," says Madame Quincy, and grandfather of Rev. Mark Hopkins, D.D., perhaps the most illustrious president of the college founded by Madame Dwight's family.

The intermarriage of the Williamses, Dwights, and Hopkinses formed a fine, aristocratic circle, into which the Sedgwicks were not very cordially welcomed. " My mother's family (of this," says Mrs. Sedgwick, " I have rather an indefinite impression than any knowledge) objected to my father on the score of family, they priding themselves on their gentle blood; but as he afterwards rose far beyond their highest water-mark, the objection was cast into oblivion by those who made it."

A few years after this marriage, the war of the Revolution began. Mr. Sedgwick entered the army, served as an officer under Washington, whose acquaintance and favor he enjoyed, and from that time, for forty years until his death, he was in public life, in positions of responsibility and honor. He was member of the Continental Congress, member of the House of Representatives, Speaker of the House, Senator from Massachusetts, and, at his death, judge of the Massachusetts Supreme Court.

Judge Sedgwick was a staunch Federalist and, in spite of the fact that he himself was not born in the purple, he shared the common Federalist contempt for the masses. "I remember my father," says Miss Sedgwick, "one of the kindest-hearted men and most observant of the rights of all beneath him, habitually spoke of the people as 'Jacobins,' 'sans-culottes,' and 'miscreants.' He — and this I speak as a type of the Federalist party — dreaded every upward step they made, regarding their elevation as a depression, in proportion to their ascension, of the intelligence and virtue of the country." "He was born too soon," says his daughter apologetically, "to relish the freedoms of democracy, and I have seen his brow lower when a free and easy mechanic came to the front door, and upon one occasion, I remember his turning off the east steps (I am sure not kicking, but the demonstration was unequivocal) a grown up lad who kept his hat on after being told to remove it." In these days one would hardly tell him to remove it, let alone hustling him off the steps.

The incident shows how far education, prosperity, wealth, and forty years of public life had transformed the father of Miss Sedgwick from the country boy of a hill-farm in Connecticut. More to our present purpose, the apologetic way in which Miss Sedgwick speaks of these high-bred prejudices of her father, shows that she does not share them. "The Federalists," she says, "stood upright, and their feet firmly planted on the rock of aristocracy but that rock was bedded in the sands, or rather was a boulder from the Old World, and the tide of democracy was surely and swiftly undermining it."

When this was written, Miss Sedgwick had made the discovery that, while the Federalists had the better "education, intellectual and moral," the "democrats had among them much native sagacity" and an earnest "determination to work out the theories of the government." She is writing to her niece: "All this my dear Alice, as you may suppose, is an after-thought. Then I entered fully, and with the faith and ignorance of childhood, into the prejudices of the time." Those prejudices must have been far behind her when her first story was written, "A New England Tale," in which it happens, inadvertently we may believe, all the worst knaves are blue-blooded and at least most of the decent persons are poor and humble. Later we shall see her slumming in New York like a Sister of Charity, 'saving those that are lost,' a field of labor toward which her Federalist education scarcely led.

She could have learned some condescension and humanity from her mother who, in spite of her fine birth, seems to have been modest and retiring to a degree. She was very reluctant to have her husband embark upon a public career; had, her daughter says, " No sympathy with what is called honor and distinction "; and wrote her husband a letter of protest which is worth quoting if only to show how a well-trained wife would write her doting husband something more than a century ago: " Pardon me, my dearest Mr. Sedgwick, if I beg you once more to think over the matter before you embark in public business. I grant that the ' call of our country,' the ' voice of fame,' and the ' Honorable' and ' Right-Honorable,' are high sounding words. ' They play around the head, but they come not near the heart.' " However, if he decides for a public career, she will submit: " Submission is my duty, and however hard, I will try to practice what reason teaches me I am under obligation to do." That address, " my dearest Mr. Sedgwick," from a wife a dozen years after marriage, shows a becoming degree of respect.

We may be sure that this gentle mother would have encouraged no silly notions of social distinctions in the minds of her children. Even Mr. Sedgwick seems to have had a softer and more human side to his nature than we have yet seen. Miss Sedgwick enjoys repeating a story which she heard from a then " venerable missionary." The son of the village shoemaker, his first upward step was as boy-of-all-work of the clerk of courts. He had driven his master to the court session in dignified silence, broken on arrival by a curt order to take in the trunk. "As he set it down in the entry," says Miss Sedgwick, " my father, then judge of the Supreme Judicial Court, was coming down stairs, bringing his trunk himself. He set it down, accosted the boy most kindly, and gave him his cordial hand. The lad's feelings, chilled by his master's haughtiness, at once melted, and took an impression of my father's kindness that was never effaced."

The individual is so much a creature of his environment, that I must carry these details a little farther. Forty years in public life, Judge

Sedgwick had an extended acquaintance and, according to the custom of the time, kept open house. "When I remember," says Miss Sedgwick, "how often the great gate swung open for the entrance of traveling vehicles, the old mansion seems to me much more like an hostelrie of the olden time than the quiet house it now is. My father's hospitality was unbounded. It extended from the gentleman in his coach, chaise, or on horseback, according to his means or necessities, to the poor, lame beggar that would sit half the night roasting at the kitchen fire with the negro servants. My father was in some sort the chieftain of his family, and his home was their resort and resting-place. Uncles and aunts always found a welcome there; cousins wintered and summered with us. Thus hospitality was an element in our education. It elicited our faculties of doing and suffering. It smothered the love and habit of minor comforts and petty physical indulgences that belong to a higher state of civilization and generate selfishness, and it made regard for others, and small sacrifices for them, a habit."

Just one word more about this home, the like of which it would be hard to find in our generation: "No bickering or dissention was ever permitted. Love was the habit, the life of the household rather than the law.— A querulous tone, a complaint, a slight word of dissention, was met by that awful frown of my father's. Jove's thunder was to a pagan believer but as a summer day's drifting cloud to it. It was not so dreadful because it portended punishment,— it was punishment; it was a token of suspension of the approbation and love that were our life."

These passages have a twofold value. They tell us in what school Miss Sedgwick was educated, and they give us a specimen of her literary style. Language is to her a supple instrument, and she makes the reader see what she undertakes to relate.

Judge Sedgwick died in Boston, in 1813, when Miss Sedgwick was twenty-three. The biographical Dictionaries say he was a member of Dr. Channing's church. As Miss Sedgwick relates the facts, he had long desired to " make a public profession of religion," but had been deterred because he could not conscientiously join the church of his family, in Stockbridge, with its Calvinistic confession, and was too tender of the feelings of his pastor to join another,— " unworthy motives," says Miss Sedgwick. Briefly stated, he now sent for Dr. Channing and received from him the communion. Later, Miss Sedgwick followed him into the Unitarian fellowship. She, and two distinguished brothers, were among the founders of the first Unitarian church in New York city.

Miss Dewey calls her volume " The Life and Letters " of Miss Sedgwick, but the Life is very scantily written. She has given us a picture rather than a biography. Indeed, to write a biography of Miss Sedgwick is no easy task, there was so much of worth in her character and so little of dramatic incident in her career. Independent in her circumstances, exempt from struggle for existence or for social position, unambitious for literary fame and surprised at its coming, unmarried and yet domestic in tastes and habits, at home in any one of the five households of her married brothers and sisters, she lived for seventy-seven years as a favored guest at the table of fortune. She saw things happen to others, but they did not happen to her. It was with her as with Whittier's sweet Quakeress:

> " For all her quiet life flowed on
>   As meadow streamlets flow,
> Where fresher green reveals alone
>   The noiseless ways they go."

Of her outward career, Miss Dewey truly says: " No striking incidents, no remarkable occurrences will be found in it, but the gradual unfolding and ripening amid congenial surroundings of a true and beautiful soul, a clear and refined intellect, and a singularly sympathetic social nature. She was born eighty years ago " —this was written in 1871,—" when the atmosphere was still electric with the storm in which we took our place among the nations, and, passing her childhood in the seclusion of a New England valley, while yet her family was linked to the great world without by ties both political and social, early and deep foundations were laid in her character of patriotism, religious feeling, love of nature, and strong attachment to home, and to those who made it what it was. And when in later life, she took her place among the acknowledged leaders of literature and society, these remained the central features of her character, and around them gathered all the graceful culture, the active philanthropy, the social accomplishment, which made her presence a joy wherever it came."

It is not singular if she began her existence at a somewhat advanced stage. She was quite sure she remembered incidents that took place before she was two years old. She remembered a dinner party at which Miss Susan Morton, afterward Madame Quincy, was present, and to which her father and her brother, Theodore, came from Philadelphia. If you are anxious to know what incidents of such an event would fix themselves in the mind of a child of two, they were these: She made her first attempt to say " Theodore," and " Philadelphia," and she tried her baby trick of biting her glass, for which she had doubtless been reproved, and watched its effect upon her father. " I recall perfectly the feeling with which I turned my eye to him, expecting to see that brow cloud with displeasure, but it was smooth as love could make it. That consciousness, that glance, that assurance, remained stamped indelibly."

" Education in the common sense," says Miss Sedgwick, " I had next to none." For schools, she fared like other children in Stockbridge, with the difference that her father was " absorbed in political life, her mother, in Catharine's youth an invalid, died early, and no one, she says, " dictated my studies or overlooked my progress. I remember feeling an intense ambition to be at the head of my class, and generally being there. Our minds were not weakened by too much study; reading, spelling, and Dwight's geography were the only paths of knowledge into which we were led;" to which accomplishments she adds as an after-thought, grammar and arithmetic.

Nevertheless, when in 1838, six of the Sedgwick family travelled together through France and Italy, doing much of those sunny lands on foot, Miss Sedgwick was interpreter for the party in both countries, apparently easy mistress of their respective languages. It is remarkable what fine culture seems to have been attainable by a New England child born more than a hundred years ago, when Harvard and Yale were, as we are told, mere High Schools, and Radcliffe and Wellesley were not even dreamed of. Instead of Radcliffe or Wellesley, Miss Sedgwick attended a boarding school in Albany, at the age of thirteen and, at the age of fifteen, another in Boston, the latter for six months, and the former could not have been more than two years. Both, according to her, gave her great social advantages, and did little for her scholarship. Miss Bell, the head of the Albany school, " rose late, was half the time out of the school, and did very little when in it."

Miss Paine's school in Boston, let us hope,

was better; but " I was at the most susceptible age. My father's numerous friends in Boston opened their doors to me. I was attractive in my appearance "— she is writing this to a niece and it is probably all true —" and, from always associating on equal terms with those much older than myself, I had a mental maturity rather striking, and with an ignorance of the world, a romantic enthusiasm, an aptitude at admiring and loving that altogether made me an object of general interest. I was admired and flattered. Harry and Robert were then resident graduates at Cambridge. They were too inexperienced to perceive the mistake I was making; they were naturally pleased with the attentions I was receiving. The winter passed away in a series of bewildering gayeties. I had talent enough to be liked by my teachers, and good nature to secure their good will. I gave them very little trouble in any way. When I came home from Boston I felt the deepest mortification at my waste of time and money, though my father never said one word to me on the subject. For the only time in my life I rose early to read French, and in a few weeks learned more by myself than I had acquired all winter."

It will be seen that she had the ability to study

without a teacher, and that is an art which, with time at one's disposal and the stimulus at hand, assures education. Intellectual stimulus was precisely what her home furnished. "I was reared in an atmosphere of high intelligence. My father had uncommon mental vigor. So had my brothers. Their daily habits and pursuits and pleasures, were intellectual, and I naturally imbibed from them a kindred taste. Their talk was not of beeves, nor of making money; that now universal passion had not entered into men and possessed them as it does now, or if it had, it was not in the sanctuary of our home,— there the money-changers did not come."

The more we know of her home life, the less wonder we have at her mental development. She says that " at the age of eight, my father, whenever he was at home, kept me up and at his side till nine o'clock in the evening, to listen to him while he read aloud to the family Hume, or Shakspere, or Don Quixote, or Hudibras. Certainly I did not understand them, but some glances of celestial light reached my soul, and I caught from his magnetic sympathy some elevation of feeling, and that love of reading which has been to me an education." A

modern girl is liable to nervous prostration
without being kept up till nine on such juvenile
literature as Hume and Shakspere at the age
of eight; but Miss Sedgwick was a country girl
who, in youth, lived out of doors and romped
like a boy and, at the age of fifty, led a party
of young nieces through France, Switzerland,
and Italy, much of the way on foot and always
at their head. Always fortune's favorite, she
enjoyed among other things remarkably good
health.

She thinks she was ten years old when she
read Rollin's Ancient History, spending the
noon intermission, when of course she ought to
have been at play, out of sight under her desk,
where she " read, and munched, and forgot myself in Cyrus's greatness."

A winter in New York, where she afterward
spent so much of her time, was her first absence
from home. She had a married sister there
whose husband was in government employ, and
her oldest brother was there studying law.
She was eleven years old; the date was 1801;
and her business in New York seems to have
been to attend a French Dancing School of
which at that era there was but one in the city.
She saw her first play, and used to dry the still

damp newspaper, in her eagerness to read the theatre announcements. She also experienced a very severe humiliation. She, with her brother, Theodore, attended a large dinner party at the house of a friend of her father. " Our host asked me, the only stranger guest, which part of a huge turkey, in which he had put his carving fork, I would take. I knew only one point of manners for such occasions, dear Alice,— that I must specify some part, and as ill luck would have it, the side-bone came first into my head, and ' Side-bone, sir,' I said. Oh what a lecture I got when we got home, the wretched little chit that compelled a gentleman to cut up a whole turkey to serve her! I cried myself to sleep that night." It was too bad to spoil that dinner party for the little girl.

Her mother died when Miss Sedgwick was seventeen; her father when she was twenty-three. All her brothers and sisters were married and living, three of them in New York city, one in Albany, and one, her youngest brother, in Lenox. With this brother in Lenox, Miss Sedgwick for many happy years, had her home, at least her summer home, having five rooms in an annex to his house built for her, into which she gathered her household gods and where she dispensed hospitality to her friends. For many years, New York city was generally her winter home.

Theoretically, we have arrived with this maiden at the age of twenty-three, but we must go back and read from one or two early letters. She is ten years old when, under date of 1800, she writes her father: " My dear papa,— Last week I received a letter from you which gave me inexpressible pleasure." This is the child's prattle of a girl of ten summers. She writes very circumspectly for her years of a new brother-in-law: " I see — indeed I think I see in Mr. Watson everything that is amiable. I am very much pleased with him; indeed we all are." The following is dated 1801, when she is eleven: " You say in your last letters that the time will soon come when you will take leave of Congress forever. That day shall I, in my own mind, celebrate forever; yes, as long as I live I shall reflect upon the dear time when my dear papa left a public life to live in a retired one with his dear wife and children; then you will have the pleasure to think, when you quit the doors of the House, that you are going to join your family forever; but, my dear papa, I cannot feel as you will when looking back on your past life in Congress.   You will remember how much you have exerted yourself in order to save your country."

There was something in the relations of this Sedgwick family, not perhaps without parallel, but very beautiful.   These brothers and sisters write to each other like lovers.   To her brother Robert, Miss Sedgwick writes, " I have just finished, my dear brother, the second perusal of your kind letter received to-day. . . . I do love my brothers with perfect devotedness, and they are such brothers as may put gladness into a sister's spirit. . . . Never, my dear Robert, did brother and sister have a more ample experience of the purity of love, and the sweet exchange of offices of kindness that binds hearts indissolubly together."

There are three letters from Robert Sedgwick to show how he reciprocated this affection. He says: " I can never be sufficiently grateful to my Maker for having given me such a sister. If I had no other sin to answer for than that of being so unworthy of her as I am, it would be more than I can bear, and yet when I read your letters I almost think that I am what I should be.   I know I have a strong aspiration to be such, and I am sure they make me better as well as happier." Again, he says: "Thanks, thanks — how cold a word, my dearest Kate, in return for your heart-cheering letter! It came to me in the midst of my Nol Pros., special verdicts, depositions, protests, business correspondence, etc., like a visitant from the skies. Indeed, my dearest Kate, you may laugh at me if you will for saying so, but there is something about your influence over me which seems to have shuffled off this mortal coil of earthiness; to be unmixed with anything that remains to be perfected; to be perfectly spiritualized, and yet to retain its contact with every part of its subject. . . . Lest I should talk foolishly on this subject, I will dismiss it, only begging you not to forget how your letters cheer, rejoice, elevate, renovate me."

Here is a love-letter from Theodore, her eldest brother: "Having this moment perused your letter the third time, I could not help giving you an answer to it, though there be nothing in it interrogative. Nor was it meant to be tender or sentimental, or learned, but like all your letters, it is so sweet, so excellent, so natural, so much without art, and yet so much beyond art, that, old, cold, selfish, unthankful as I am, the tears are in my eyes, and I thank

God that I have such a sister." Let us revenge ourselves upon these brother and sister lovers by saying that perhaps they did not feel any more than some other people, only they had a habit of expressing their feelings. If that was all, we cannot deny that the habit was very beautiful.

Why did Miss Sedgwick never marry? We are not distinctly told; but she did not need to, with such lovers in her own family. Besides, how could she find any one, in her eyes, equal to those brothers, and how could she marry any one of lower merit? " I am satisfied," she writes, " by long and delightful experience, that I can never love any body better than my brothers. I have no expectation of ever finding their equal in worth and attraction, therefore — do not be alarmed; I am not on the verge of a vow of celibacy, nor have I the slightest intention of adding any rash resolutions to the ghosts of those that have been frightened to death by the terrors of maiden life; but therefore — I shall never change my condition until I change my mind." This is at the age of twenty-three.

Later in life, after many changes had come, she seems to have wished she had not been so very hard to suit. Fifteen years roll away, during which we see one suitor after another, dismissed, when she writes in a journal not to be read in her life-time, " It is difficult for one who began life as I did, the primary object of affection to many, to come by degrees to be first to none, and still to have my love remain in its full strength, and craving such returns as have no substitute. . . . It is the necessity of a solitary condition, an unnatural state. . . . From my own experience I would not advise any one to remain unmarried, for my experience has been a singularly happy one. My feelings have never been embittered by those slights and taunts that the repulsive and neglected have to endure; there has been no period of my life to the present moment when I might not have allied myself respectably, and to those sincerely attached to me. . . . I have troops of friends, some devotedly attached to me, and yet the result of this very happy experience is that there is no substitute for those blessings which Providence has placed first, and ordained that they shall be purchased at the dearest sacrifice." Those who have paid the price and purchased the blessings may have the satisfaction of knowing that, according to Miss Sedgwick's mature opinion, they have chosen the better part.

We might call this statement the Confessions of an Old Maid who might have done better. She closes her testimony with an acknowledgment that she " ought to be grateful and humble," and the " hope, through the grace of God, to rise more above the world, to attain a higher and happier state of feeling, to order my house for that better world where self may lose something of its engrossing power." This religious attitude was not unusual, nor merely conventional and unmeaning. All the Sedgwick family seem to have been constitutionally religious. The mother was almost painfully meek in her protest against her husband's embarking upon a public career; Mr. Sedgwick has been deterred from joining a church only by some impossible articles of puritan divinity, but cannot die happy until he has received the communion from Dr. Channing; " both my sisters were very religious," says Miss Sedgwick; while the letters I have quoted from two of her brothers, young lawyers and men of the world, have the devoutness of the psalms. " I can never be sufficiently grateful to my Maker for having given me such a sister," says Robert; and Theodore: "selfish, unthankful as I am, the tears are in my eyes, and I thank God that I have such a sister." Of course one can use a religious dialect without meaning much by it, but these Sedgwicks were cultivated people, who thought for themselves, and did not speak cant to each other.

Since it was a religious impulse that turned Miss Sedgwick's mind to literature, it is worth while to follow the thread of her spiritual history. This was written at the age of twenty when she was looking for a religious experience that never came, and would have considered herself one of the wicked: "On no subject would I voluntarily be guilty of hypocricy, and on that which involves all the importance of our existence I should shrink from the slightest insincerity. You misunderstood my last letter. I exposed to you a state of mind and feeling produced, not by religious impressions, but by the convictions of reason." Of course "reason" was no proper organ of religion; but besides this defect, her interest in serious things was liable to interruption "by the cares and pleasures of the world" and, perhaps worst of all, "I have not a fixed belief on some of the most material points of our religion." One does not see how a person in this state of mind should have anything to call "our religion." She seems to have advanced much further in a letter to her brother Robert, three years later: "I long to see you give your testimony of your acceptance of the forgiving love of your Master. . . . God grant, in his infinite mercy, that we may all touch the garment of our Savior's righteousness and be made whole."

The editor of these letters tells us that Miss Sedgwick is now a member of Dr. Mason's church in New York city, having joined at the age of twenty, or soon after the letter in which she says she is not satisfied on certain points of doctrine. Dr. Mason is described as an undiluted Calvinist, "who then was the most conspicuous pulpit orator in the country — a man confident in his faith and bold to audacity." Miss Sedgwick stands the strong meat of Calvinism ten years, when we have this letter. "I presume you saw the letter I wrote Susan, in which I said that I did not think I should go to Dr. Mason's Church again. . . . You know, my dear Frances, that I never adopted some of the articles of the creed of that church and some of those upon which the doctor is fond of expatiating, and which appear to me both unscriptural and very unprofitable, and, I think, very demoralizing."

What perhaps stimulated the zeal of Dr. Mason to insist upon doctrines always objectionable to Miss Sedgwick, was an attempt then being made to establish a Unitarian church in New York city. She has not joined in the movement, but does not know but it may come to that. It is a critical moment in Miss Sedgwick's history, and it happened at this time she went to hear Dr. Mason's farewell sermon. " As usual," she says, " he gave the rational Christians an anathema. He said they had fellowship with the devil: no, he would not slander the devil, they were worse, etc." Very possibly this preaching had its proper effect upon many hearers, and they gave the " rational Christians " a wide berth, but it precipitated Miss Sedgwick into their ranks. She was not then a thorough-going Unitarian, saying, " there are some of your articles of unbelief that I am not Protestant enough to subscribe to "; a little more gentleness on the part of Dr. Mason could have kept her, but she could not stand " what seems to me," she says, " a gross violation of the religion of the Redeemer, and an insult to a large body of Christians entitled to respect and affection."

She joined the tabooed circle in 1821, and wrote from Stockbridge, " Some of my friends here have, as I learn, been a little troubled, but after the crime of confessed Unitarianism, nothing can surprise them "; she longs to look upon a Christian minister who does not regard her as " a heathen and a publican." An aunt, very fond of her, said to her, one day as they were parting, " Come and see me as often as you can, dear, for you know, after this world we shall never meet again."

These religious tribulations incited her to write a short story, after the parable of the Pharisee and the Publican, to contrast two kinds of religion, of one of which she had seen more than was good. The story was to appear as a tract, but it outgrew the dimensions of a tract, and was published as a book under the title of " A New England Tale." It is not a masterpiece of literature but, like all of Miss Sedgwick's works, it contains some fine delineations of character and vivid descriptions of local scenery. It can be read to-day with interest and pleasure. As a dramatic presentation of the self-righteous and the meek, in a New

England country town a century ago, it is very effective. " Mrs. Wilson " is perhaps a more stony heart than was common among the ' chosen vessels of the Lord,' but so the Pharisee in the parable may have been a trifle exaggerated. The advantage of this kind of writing is that you do not miss the point of the story.

Miss Dewey says The New England Tale gave Miss Sedgwick an " immediate position in the world of American literature." Her brother Theodore wrote, " It exceeds all my expectations, fond and flattering as they were "; her brother Harry, " I think, dear Kate, that your destiny is fixed. As you are such a Bible-ist, I only say don't put your light under a bushel." That the book did not fall still-born is evident when he says further, "The orthodox do all they can to put it down." On the other hand, her publisher wanted to print a cheap edition of 3,000 copies for missionary purposes. I should like to see that done to-day by some zealous liberal-minded publisher.

The New England Tale appeared in 1822, when Cooper had only published " Precaution " and " The Spy." In 1824, Miss Sedgwick published " Redwood," of which a second edition was

called for the same year, and which was republished in England and translated into French.
It reached distinction in the character of De-
borah Lenox, of which Miss Edgworth said,
" It is to America what Scott's characters are
to Scotland, valuable as original pictures."
Redwood was reviewed by Bryant in the North
American, in an article which, he says, was up
to that time his " most ambitious attempt in
prose." " Hope Leslie " appeared in 1827. It
was so much better than its predecessors, said
the *Westminster Review*, that one would not
suppose it by the same hand. Sismondi, the
Swiss historian, wrote the author a letter of
thanks and commendation, which was followed
by a life-long friendship between these two authors. Mrs. Child, then Miss Francis and the
author of " Hobomok " and " The Rebels,"
wrote her that she had nearly completed a story
on Capt. John Smith which now she will not dare
to print, but she surrenders with less reluctance,
she says, " for I love my conqueror." " Is not
that beautiful? " says Miss Sedgwick. " Better to write and to feel such a sentiment than to
indite volumes."

" Clarence " was published in 1830, and I am
glad to say, she sold the rights to the first edi-

tion for $1,200, before the critics got hold of it. The scene is laid in New York and in high life. The story, said the *North American Review*, is "improbable" but not "dull." Miss Dewey says, "It is the most romantic and at the same time the wittiest of her novels," but Bryant says it has been the least read. "The Linwoods, or Sixty Years Since in America," appeared in 1835, and Bryant called it "a charming tale of home life, thought by many to be the best of her novels properly so called."

If Miss Sedgwick had written none of these more elaborate works, she would deserve a permanent place in our literature for a considerable library of short stories, among which I should name "A Berkshire Tradition," a pathetic tale of the Revolution; "The White Scarf," a romantic story of Mediæval France; "Fanny McDermot," a study of conventional morality; "Home," of which the *Westminster Review* said, "We wish this book was in the hands of every mechanic in England"; "The Poor Rich Man and the Rich Poor Man" of which Joseph Curtis, the philanthropist, said, "in all his experiences he had never known so much good fruit from the publication of any book"; and, not least, "Live and let Live: or domestic service illustrated," of which Dr. Channing wrote, " I cannot, without violence to my feelings, refrain from expressing to you the great gratification with which I have read your ' Live and let Live.' Thousands will be better and happier for it. . . . Your three last books, I trust, form an era in our literature."

This was high praise, considering that there was then no higher literary authority in America than Dr. Channing. .However, a message from Chief Justice Marshall, through Judge Story, belongs with it: ' Tell her I have read with great pleasure everything she has written, and wish she would write more." She had gained an enviable position in literature and she had done a great deal of useful work during the fifteen years since the timid appearance of " A New England Tale," but she seems to have regarded her books as simply a " by-product ": " My author existence has always seemed something accidental, extraneous, and independent of my inner self. My books have been a pleasant occupation and excitement in my life. . . . But they constitute no portion of my happiness — that is, of such as I derive from the dearest relations of life. When I feel that my writings have made any one hap-

pier or better, I feel an emotion of gratitude to
Him who has made me the medium of any blessing to my fellow creatures."

In 1839, Miss Sedgwick went to Europe in
company with her brother Robert, and other
relatives. The party was abroad two years
and, on its return, Miss Sedgwick collected her
European letters and published them in two
volumes. They give one a view of Europe as
seen by an intelligent observer still in the first
half of the last century. She breakfasted with
Rogers, the banker and poet, with whom she met
Macaulay whose conversation was to her " rich
and delightful. Some might think he talks too
much; but none, except from their own impatient vanity, could wish it were less." She had
tea at Carlyle's, found him " simple, natural
and kindly, his conversation as picturesque as
his writings." She " had an amusing evening
at Mr. Hallam's "; he made her " quite forget
he was the sage of the ' Middle Ages.' " At
Hallam's she met Sydney Smith who was " in
the vein, and we saw him, I believe, to advantage. His wit is not, as I expected, a succession of brilliant explosions but a sparkling
stream of humor."

In Geneva, she visited her friends, the Sismondis, and in Turin received a call from Silvio Pellico, martyr to Italian liberty. " He is of low stature and slightly made, a sort of etching of a man with delicate and symmetrical features, just enough body to gravitate and keep the spirit from its natural upward flight — a more shadowy Dr. Channing."

Soon after Miss Sedgwick's return from Europe, she became connected with the Women's Prison Association of New York City, of which from 1848 to 1863 she was president. An extract from one letter must suffice to suggest the nature of her activities in connection with this and kindred philanthropies : " It is now just ten, and I have come up from the City Hall, in whose dismal St. Giles precincts I have been to see a colored ragged school. . . . My Sundays are not days of rest. . . . My whole soul is sickened ; and to-day when I went to church filled with people in their fine summer clothes, and heard a magnificent sermon from Dr. Dewey, and thought of the streets and dens through which I had just walked, I could have cried out, Why are ye here? "

A fellow-member of the Prison Association, who often accompanied her on her visits to hospitals and prisons, " especially the Tombs,

Blackwell's, and Randall's Island," says, " In her visitations, she was called upon to kneel at the bedside of the sick and dying. The sweetness of her spirit, and the delicacy of her nature, felt by all who came within her atmosphere, seemed to move the unfortunate to ask this office of her, and it was never asked in vain."

Always a philanthropist, Miss Sedgwick was not a "reformer" in the technical sense; that is, she did not enlist in the "movements" of her generation, for Temperance, or Anti-Slavery, or Woman's Rights. She shrunk from the excesses of the "crusaders," but she was never slow in striking a blow in a good cause. " Uncle Tom's Cabin " was published in 1852, but its indictment of slavery is not more complete than Miss Sedgwick made in " Redwood," her second novel, twenty-five years before. A planter's boy sees a slave starved to famishing and then whipped to death. It hurt his boy heart, but he afterward became hardened to such necessary severity and he tells the story to a fellow planter with apologies for his youthful sentimentality. Does " Uncle Tom's Cabin " show more clearly the two curses of slavery:

cruelty to the slave and demoralization to the master?

She sympathized with the abolitionists in their purpose but not always with their methods: " The great event of the past week has been the visit of the little apostle of Abolitionism — Lucy Stone." This was in 1849 when Mrs. Stone was thirty-one. " She has one of the very sweetest voices I ever heard, a readiness of speech and grace that furnish the external qualifications of an orator — a lovely countenance too — and the intensity, entire forgetfulness and the divine calmness that fit her to speak in the great cause she has undertaken." But in spite of this evident sympathy with the purpose of the Abolitionists, Miss Sedgwick declined to attend a meeting of the Anti-Slavery Society, saying: " It seemed to me that so much had been intemperately said, so much rashly urged, on the death of that noble martyr, John Brown, by the Abolitionists, that it was not right to appear among them as one of them."

Not even Lucy Stone, however, could have felt more horror at the institution of slavery. The Compromise Measures of 1850 made her shudder: " my hands are cold as ice; the blood has curdled in my heart; that word *compromise* has a bad savor when truth and right are in question." When the Civil War came, in her seventieth year, she had " an intense desire to live to see the conclusion of the struggle," but could not conjecture " how peace and good neighborhood are ever to follow from this bitter hate." " It is delightful to see the gallantry of some of our men, who are repeating the heroic deeds that seemed fast receding to fabulous times." Some of these young heroes were very near to her. Maj. William Dwight Sedgwick, who fell on the bloody field of Antietam was her nephew, Gen. John Sedgwick, killed at the battle of Spottsylvania, was her cousin.

As she was not in the Anti-Slavery crusade, so she was not in the Woman's Rights crusade. She wished women to have a larger sphere, and she did much to enlarge the sphere of her sex, but it was by taking it and making it, rather than by talking about it. " Your *might* must be your *right*," she says in a chapter on The Rights of Women, in " Means and Ends." Voting did not seem to her a function suited to women: " I cannot believe it was ever intended that women should lead armies, harangue in halls of legislation, bustle up to ballot-boxes, or sit on judicial tribunals." The gentle Lucy Stone would not have considered this argument conclusive, but it satisfied Miss Sedgwick.

In 1857, after a silence of twenty-two years, in which only short stories and one or two biographies came from her hand, she published another two-volume novel entitled, " Married or Single." It is perhaps her best work; at least it has been so considered by many readers. She was then sixty-seven and, though she had ten more years to live, they were years of declining power. These last years were spent at the home of her favorite niece, Mrs. William Minot, Jr., in West Roxbury, Mass., and there tenderly and reverently cared for, she died in 1867.

Bryant, who was her life-long friend, and who, at her instance wrote some of his hymns, gives this estimate of her character: " Admirable as was her literary life, her home life was more so; and beautiful as were the examples set forth in her writings, her own example was, if possible, still more beautiful. Her unerring sense of rectitude, her love of truth, her ready sympathy, her active and cheerful beneficence, her winning and gracious manners, the perfection of high breeding, make up a character, the idea of which, as it rests in my mind, I would not exchange for anything in her own interesting works of fiction."

II
MARY LOVELL WARE

MARY LOVELL WARE

Of all the saints in the calendar of the Church there is no name more worthy of the honor than that of Mary Lovell Ware. The college of cardinals, which confers the degree of sainthood for the veneration of faithful Catholics, will never recognize her merits and encircle her head with a halo, but when the list of Protestant saints is made up, the name of Mary L. Ware will be in it, and among the first half dozen on the scroll.

The writer was a student in the Divinity School at Cambridge when a classmate commended to him the Memoirs of Mrs. Ware as one of the few model biographies. It was a book not laid down in the course of study; its reading was postponed for that convenient season for which one waits so long; but he made a mental note of the " Memoirs of Mary L. Ware," which many years did not efface. There is a book one must read, he said to himself, if he would die happy.

Mrs. Ware's maiden name was Pickard.   To

the end of her days, when she put herself in a
pillory as she often did, she called herself by her
maiden name. "That," she would say, "was
Mary Pickard." I infer that she thought
Mary Pickard had been a very bad girl.

Her mother's name was Lovell,— Mary Lovell, — granddaughter of "Master Lovell," long
known as a classical teacher in colonial Boston,
and daughter of James Lovell, an active Revol-
utionist, a prominent member of the Continental Congress and, from the end of the war
to his death, Naval officer in the Boston Custom
House. Mr. Lovell had eight sons, one of
whom was a successful London merchant, and
one daughter, who remained with her parents
until at twenty-five she married Mr. Pickard
and who, when her little girl was five years old
returned, as perhaps an only daughter should,
to take care of her parents in their old age.
So it happened that the childhood of Mrs.
Ware was passed at her grandfather Lovell's,
in Pearl St., Boston, then an eligible place of
residence.

Mr. Pickard was an Englishman by birth,
and a merchant with business connections in
London and Boston, between which cities, for a
time, his residence alternated. Not much is

MARY LOVELL WARE

said of him in the Memoirs, beyond the fact
that he was an Episcopalian with strong attachment to the forms of his church, as an
Englishman might be expected to be.

Of Mrs. Pickard we learn more. She is said
to have possessed a vigorous mind, to have been
well educated and a fine conversationalist, with
a commanding figure, benignant countenance,
and dignified demeanor, so that one said of her,
" She seems to have been born for an empress."
Like her husband she was an Episcopalian
though, according to the Memoirs, less strenu-
ously Episcopalian than Mr. Pickard. She
had been reared in a different school. Her
father,— Mr. James Lovell — we are told, was
a free-thinker, or as the Memoirs put it,
" had adopted some infidel principles." and
" treated religion with little respect in his family." The " infidels " of that day were generally good men, only they were not orthodox.
Jefferson, Madison, Franklin and Washington
were such infidels. After Channing's day, this
kind of man here in New England was absorbed
by the Unitarian movement, and, as a separate
class, disappeared. Mrs. Pickard was bred in
this school and she appears never to have forgotten her home training. " She was unosten-

tatious and charitable," says an early friend,
" and her whole life was an exhibition of the
ascendency of *principle* over mere taste and
feeling."

Her religious attitude becomes interesting,
because in an exceptional degree, she formed her
remarkable daughter,— who was an only child
and until the age of thirteen had no teacher
except this forceful and level-headed mother.

With these antecedents, Mary Lovell Pickard
was born in Boston, October 2, 1798, John
Adams being then President. In 1802, Mary
having passed her third summer, Mr. Pickard's
business called him to London, where he resided
with his family two years, so that the child's
fifth birthday was duly celebrated in mid-ocean
on the homeward voyage. In a letter of Mrs.
Pickard, written during this London residence,
she says, " Mr. Pickard is even more anxious
than I to go home. Mary is the only contented
one. She is happy all the time." There is so
much that is sad in this record that, before we
have done, the reader will be glad the little girl
had at least a bright and sunny childhood to remember. It appears she did remember it. It
may not be remarkable, but it is interesting, that
the experiences of this early London life,— be-

tween her third and fifth year,— made an indelible impression upon her, so that twenty years later when she was again in England, much to her own delight, she " recognized her old London home and other objects with which she was then familiar."

A lady who was a fellow passenger of the Pickards on their homeward voyage was struck by the gentle management of the mother and the easy docility of the child. To say, " It will make me unhappy if you do that," was an extreme exercise of maternal authority, to which the child yielded unresisting obedience. This, of course, is told to the credit of the child, but the merit, probably belongs to the mother. Doubtless we could all have such children if we were that kind of a parent. A little tact, unfailing gentleness, and an infinite self control: with these, it would seem one may smile and kiss a child into an angel.

On arriving in Boston, Mrs. Pickard took her family to her father's, where she remained until her death, and where, we read, " with parents and grandparents, Mary found a home whose blessings filled her heart." Being an only child, with four elderly persons, Mary was likely to be too much petted or too much fretted. We are glad to know that she was not fretted or over-trained. In a letter of retrospect, she writes, " For many years a word of blame never reached my ears." An early friend of the family writes, " It has been said that Mary was much indulged; and I believe it may be said so with truth. But she was not indulged in idleness, selfishness, and rudeness; she was indulged in healthful sports, in pleasant excursions, and in companionship with other children."

Everything went smoothly with her until the age of ten when, rather earlier than most children, she discovered her conscience: " At ten years of age I waked up to a sense of the danger of the state of indulgence in which I was living "; but let us hope the crisis was not acute. It does not seem to have been. According to the testimony of her first teacher, she was simply precocious morally, but not at all morbid. Her school was at Hingham, whither she was sent at the age of thirteen. The teacher says that with her " devotedness to the highest objects and purposes of our existence, she was one of the most lively and playful girls among her companions, and a great favorite with them all."

There seems to have been really no cloud upon her existence up to this point,— the age of thirteen. I have had a reason for dwelling upon this charming period of her childhood, untroubled by a cloud, because from this date until her death, the hand of God seems to have been very heavy upon her, afflictions fell upon her like rain, and it required a brave spirit to carry the burdens appointed for her to bear. Happily, she had a brave spirit, did not know that her life was hard, " gloried in tribulation," like St. Paul, and was never more cheerful or thankful than when she was herself an invalid, with an invalid husband to be cared for like a baby, seven children to be clothed and fed, and not enough money at the year's end to square accounts. Ruskin tells of a servant who had served his mother faithfully fifty-seven years. " She had," he says, " a natural gift and specialty for doing disagreeable things; above all, the service of the sick-room; so that she was never quite in her glory unless some of us were ill." It will be seen further on that these were only a part of the accomplishments of Mrs. Ware. It is fortunate if a woman is so made that her spirits rise as her troubles thicken, but the reader of the story will be thankful that her life was not all a battle, that her childhood was more than ordinarily serene and sunny, and that not for a dozen years at least, did she have to be a heroine in order to be happy.

Mary had been in Hingham about half a year, enjoying her school-girl life, when her mother was taken ill, fatally ill as it proved, and the child, then at the age of thirteen, was called home and installed in the sick-room as nurse. This was the beginning of sorrow. The mother lingered through the winter and died in the following May. There remained of the family, the grandparents, one son of fine talents, but of unfortunate habits, and her father, "broken in spirits and in fortune, clinging to his only child with doting and dependent affection." We can see that it could not have been a cheerful home for a young girl of thirteen. Some thirty years later, she wrote to one of her children, "I think I have felt the want all my life of a more cheerful home in my early childhood, a fuller participation in the pleasures and 'follies' of youth." I put this reflection here, because it does not apply to the years preceding the loss of her mother while it exactly fits the period that now follows.

The year following her mother's death, Mary attended a girls' school in Boston. A passage from a letter written at this period will show something of her quality. It is dated February 27, 1813, when she was fourteen and a few months. Besides, she had been at school, six months at a time, a total of about one year. She had been mentioning two or three novels, and then discourses as follows: "Novels are generally supposed to be improper books for young people, as they take up the time which ought to be employed in more useful pursuits; which is certainly very true; but as a recreation to the mind, such books as these cannot possibly do any hurt, as they are good moral lessons. Indeed, I think there is scarcely any book from which some good may not be derived; though it cannot be expected that any young person has judgment enough to leave all the bad and take only the good, when there is a great proportion of the former." Perhaps I am wrong in thinking this an exhibition of remarkable reflection and expression in a girl well under fifteen, whether she had been at school or otherwise. Mrs. Ware was always a wonderful letter-writer, though, if we take her word for it, she had little of her mother's gift as a conversationalist. It seems to have been a life-long habit to see the old year out and the new year in, spending the quiet hours in writing letters to her friends. In one of these anniversary letters, written when she was fifteen, she says; " I defy anyone to tell from my appearance that I have not everything to make me happy. I have much and am happy. My little trials are essential to my happiness." In that last sentence we have the entire woman. Her trials were always, as she thought, essential to her happiness.

On this principle, her next twelve years ought to have been very happy, since they were sufficiently full of tribulation. The two years following her mother's death, passed in the lonely home in Boston, were naturally depressing. Besides, she was born for religion, and the experience through which she had passed had created a great hunger in her soul,. Trinity Church, into which she had been baptized, had not yet passed through the hands of Phillips Brooks, and its ministrations, admirable as they are for the ordinary child, were inadequate for the wants of a thoughtful girl like Mary Pickard. The final effect was, she says, to throw her more upon herself and to compel her to seek, " by reading, meditation and prayer, to find that knowledge and stimulus to virtue which I failed to find in the ministrations of the Sabbath."

At this critical period, she returned to the school at Hingham, which she had left two years before, and there, in the Third Church, then presided over by Rev. Henry Colman, one of the fathers of the Unitarian heresy, she found peace and satisfaction to her spirit. Ten years later, she spent a week in Hingham, visiting friends and reviving, as she says, the memory of the " first awakening of my mind to high and holy thoughts and resolves. " The crisis which, elsewhere, we read of at the age of ten, was a subordinate affair. This Hingham experience, at the age of sixteen, was really the moral event in her history.

As hers was a type of religion,— she would have said " piety ",— a blend of reason and sentiment, peculiar to the Unitarianism of that generation, hardly to be found in any household of faith to-day, we must let her disclose her inner consciousness. One Saturday morning, she writes a long letter to one of her teachers saying that she feels it a duty and a privilege " to be a member of the Church of Christ," but she fears she does not understand what the relation implies, and says, " Tell me if you should consider it a violation of the sacredness of the institution, to think I might with impunity be a member of it. I am well aware of the condemnation denounced on those who *partake* unworthily." She refers to the Lord's Supper. It is to be hoped that her teacher knew enough to give the simple explanation of that dark saying of the apostle about eating unworthily. At all events, she connected herself with the church, received the communion, and was very happy. " From the moment I had decided what to do, not a feeling arose which I could wish to suppress; conscious of pure motives, all within was calm, and I wondered how I could for a moment hesitate. They were feelings I never before experienced, and for once I realized that it is only when we are at peace with ourselves that we can enjoy true happiness. . . . I could not sleep, and actually laid awake all night out of pure happiness."

After a few months, sooner than she expected, she returns to Boston and sits under the ministrations of Dr. Channing, to her an object of veneration. She writes that her heart is too

full for utterance: " It will not surprise you
that Mr. Channing's sermons are the cause; but
no account that I could give could convey any
idea of them. You have heard some of the same
class; they so entirely absorb the feelings as to
render the mind incapable of action, and consequently leave on the memory at times no distinct impression." I should like to quote all
she says of Channing, both as a revelation of
him, and of herself. She heard him read the
psalm, " What shall I render unto God for all
his mercies? " and says, " The ascription of
praise which followed was more truly sublime
than anything I ever heard or read." It must
have been an event,—it certainly was for
her,—to listen to one of Dr. Channing's
prayers: " It seems often to me, while in the
hour of prayer I give myself up to the thought
of heaven, as though I had in reality left the
world, and was enjoying what is promised to
the Christian. I fear, however, these feelings
are too often delusive; we substitute the love of
holiness for the actual possession."

There her sanity comes in to check her emo-
tionalism. She is reflecting upon another experience with Dr. Channing when she comes
very near making a criticism upon him. She

tells us that she does not mean him; he is excepted from these remarks, but she says, " There are few occasions which will authorize a minister to excite the feelings of an audience in a very great degree, and none which can make it allowable for him to rest in mere excitement." To complete the portraiture of her soul, I will take a passage from a letter written at the age of twenty-five, when death has at last stripped her of all her family, " I believe that all events that befall us are exactly such as are best adapted to improve us; and I find in a perfect confidence in the wisdom and love which I know directs them, a source of peace which no other thing can give; and in the difficulty which I find in acting upon this belief I see a weakness of nature, which those very trials are designed to assist us in overcoming, and which trial alone can conquer."

Mary Pickards were not common even in that generation, but this creed was then common, and this blend of reason and religious feeling, fearlessly called " piety," was characteristic of Channing, her teacher, and of Henry Ware, afterward her husband. It was the real " Channing Unitarianism." Pity there is no more of it.

Mary was sixteen years old,— to be exact, sixteen and a half; the serene and beautiful faith of Channing had done its perfect work upon her; and she was now ready for whatever fate, or as she would have said, Providence, might choose to send. It sent the business failure of Mr. Pickard, in which not only his own fortune was swept away but also the estate of Mr. Lovell was involved. Upon the knowledge of this disaster, Mary wrote a cheerful letter, in which she said: "I should be sorry to think you consider me so weak as to bend under a change of fortune to which all are liable." Certainly she will not bend, but she is obliged to quit school and return to the shattered home.

Before the summer was over, her grandfather, Mr. Lovell, died; whether the end was hastened by the financial embarrassments in which Mr. Pickard had involved him, is not said. Mrs. Lovell, the grandmother, followed her husband in two years,— for Mary, two years of assiduous nursing and tender care. Perhaps one sentence from a letter at this time will assist us in picturing her in this exacting service. She says that she is leading a monotonous existence, that her animal spirits are not sufficient for both duty and solitude, "And when evening closes, and my beloved charge is laid peacefully to rest, excitement ceases, and I am thrown on myself for pleasure."

With the death of the grandmother, the home was broken up, and Mary, trying to help her father do a little business without capital, went to New York city as his commercial agent. Her letters to her father are " almost exclusively business letters," and he on his part gives her " directions for the sale and purchase, not only of muslins and moreens, but also of skins, salt-petre, and the like."

Details of this period of her career are not abundant in the Memoirs, and the death of her father, in 1823, put an end to her business apprenticeship.

Apparently, she was not entirely destitute. At the time of his disaster, her father wrote, " As we calculated you would, after some time, have enough to support yourself, without mental or bodily exertion." That is, presumably, after the settlement of her grandfather's estate. As her biographer says, " Every member of her own family had gone, and she had smoothed the passage of everyone." But she had many friends, and one is tempted to say, Pity she could not have settled down in cozy quarters and made herself comfortable.

Indeed she did make a fair start. She joined a couple of friends, going abroad in search of health, for a visit to England. She had relatives on the Lovell side, in comfortable circumstances near London, and an aunt on her father's side, in the north of England, in straightened circumstances. She resolved to make the acquaintance of all these relatives.

The party arrived in Liverpool in April, 1824, and for a year and a half, during which their headquarters were in London, Paris was visited, Southern England and Wales were explored, and finally the Lovell relatives were visited and found to have good hearts and open arms. For these eighteen months, Mary Pickard's friends could have wished her no more delightful existence. She had tea with Mrs. Barbauld, heard Irving, then the famous London preacher, and saw other interesting persons and charming things in England. There is material for a very interesting chapter upon this delightful experience. It was followed by a drama of misery and horror, in which she was both spectator and actor, when young and old died around her as if smitten by pestilence, and her own vigorous constitution was irreparably broken.

This episode was vastly more interesting to her than the pleasant commonplace of travel, and much more in keeping with what seems to have been her destiny. In the autumn of her second year abroad, she went to discover her aunt, sister of Mr. Pickard, in Yorkshire. The writer of the Memoirs says that this visit " forms the most remarkable and in some respects the most interesting and important chapter of her life." She found her aunt much better than she expected, nearly overpowered with joy to see her, living in a little two story cottage of four rooms, which far exceeded anything she ever saw for neatness. The village bore the peculiarly English name of Osmotherly, and was the most primitive place she had ever been in. The inhabitants were all of one class and that the poorer class of laborers, ignorant as possible, but simple and sociable. Terrible to relate, smallpox, typhus fever, and whooping cough were at that moment epidemic in that village.

It will be impossible to put the situation before us more briefly than by quoting a passage from one of her letters: " My aunt's two daughters are married and live in this village;

one of them, with three children, has a husband
at the point of death with a fever; his brother
died yesterday of smallpox, and two of her children have the whooping-cough; added to this,
their whole dependence is upon their own exer-
tions, which are of course entirely stopped now.
. . . You may suppose, under such a state
of things, I shall find enough to do."

The death of the husband, whom of course
Miss Pickard nursed through his illness, is reported in the next letter, which contains also
this characteristic statement, " It seems to me
that posts of difficulty are my appointed lot and
my element, for I do feel lighter and happier
when I have difficulties to overcome. Could you
look in upon me you would think it impossible
that I could be even tolerably comfortable, and
yet I am cheerful, and get along as easily as
possible, and am in truth happy."

Evidently, all we can do with such a person
is to congratulate her over the most terrible experiences. In a letter five days later, the baby
dies of whooping-cough, and in her arms; a
fortnight later, the mother dies of typhus fever;
within another month, two boys, now orphans,
are down with the same fever at once, and one
of them dies. In the space of eight weeks, she

saw five persons of one family buried, and four of them she had nursed. By this time, the aunt was ill, and Miss Pickard nursed her to convalescence.

This campaign had lasted three months, and she left the scene of combat with a clear conscience. She was allowed a breathing spell of a month in which to visit some pleasant friends and recuperate her strength, when we find her back in Osmotherly again nursing her aunt. It was the end of December and she was the only servant in the house. Before this ordeal was over, she was taken ill herself, and had to be put to bed and nursed. In crossing a room, a cramp took her; she fell on the floor, lay all night in the cold, calling in vain for assistance. She did not finally escape from these terrible scenes until the end of January, five months from the time she entered them.

Miss Pickard returned to Boston after an absence of about two years and a half, during which time, as one of her friends wrote her, " You have passed such trying scenes, have so narrowly escaped, and done more, much more, than almost any body ever did before." She went away a dear school-girl friend and a valued acquaintance; she was welcomed home as a martyr fit to be canonized, and was received as a conquering heroine.

In a letter dated from Gretna Green, where so many run-away lovers have been made happy, she playfully reflects upon the possibilities of her visit, if only she had a lover, and concludes that she " must submit to single blessedness a little longer." Our sympathies would have been less taxed if she had submitted to single blessedness to the end. Why could she not now be quiet, let well enough alone, and make herself comfortable? Destiny had apparently ordered things for her quite differently. One cannot avoid his destiny, and it was her destiny to marry, and marriage was to bring her great happiness, tempered by great sorrows.

The man who was to share her happiness and her sorrows was Rev. Henry Ware, Jr., then the almost idolized minister of the Second Church, in Boston. Mr. Ware was the son of another Henry Ware, professor of theology at Harvard, whose election to the chair of theology in 1806 opened the great Unitarian controversy. Two sons of Professor Ware entered the ministry, Henry and William, the latter the first Unitarian minister settled in New York city. Rev. John F. Ware, well remembered as pastor of Arlington St. Church in Boston, was the son of Henry, so that for more than half a century, the name of Ware was a great factor in Unitarian history.

After Dr. Channing, Henry Ware was perhaps the most popular preacher in any Boston pulpit. One sermon preached by him on a New Year's eve, upon the Duty of Improvement, became memorable. In spite of a violent snow storm, the church was filled to overflowing, a delegation coming from Cambridge. Of this sermon, a hearer said: " No words from mortal lips ever affected me like those." There was a difference between Unitarian preaching then and now. That famous sermon closed like this: " I charge you, as in the presence of God, who sees and will judge you,— in the name of Jesus Christ, who beseeches you to come to him and live,— by all your hopes of happiness and life,—I charge you let not this year die, and leave you impenitent. Do not dare to utter defiance in its decaying hours. But, in the stillness of its awful midnight, prostrate yourselves penitently before your Maker; and let the morning sun rise upon you, thoughtful and serious men." One does not see how the so-called

' Evangelicals ' could have quarreled with that preaching.

Mr. Ware had been in his parish nine years, his age was thirty-two, he was in the prime of life, and at the climax of his power and his popularity. Three years before, he had been left a widower with three young children, one of whom became Rev. John F. Ware. That these two intensely religious natures, that of Mary Pickard and that of Henry Ware, should have been drawn together is not singular. In writing to his sister, Mr. Ware speaks tenderly of his late wife and says, " I have sought for the best mother to her children, and the best I have found." Late in life, one of these children said, " Surely God never gave a boy such a mother or a man such a friend."

Miss Pickard engaged to be a very docile wife. " Instead of the self-dependent self-governed being you have known me," she writes to a friend, " I have learned to look to another for guidance and happiness." She is " as happy as mortal can be." Indeed it was almost too much for earth. " It has made me," she says, " more willing to leave the world and enjoy the happiness of heaven than I ever thought I should be. Strange that a thing from which of all others,

I should have expected the very opposite effect, should have done this."

The year following the marriage of these saintly lovers,— one can call them nothing less, — was one of exceeding happiness and of immense activity to both. It is not said, but we can see that each must have been a tonic to the other. Considerate persons felt a scruple about taking any of the time of their pastor's wife. " Mrs. Ware," said one, " at home and abroad, is the busiest woman of my acquaintance," and others felt that way. Before the year ended, Mrs. Ware had a boy baby of her own to increase her occupations and her happiness. It lived a few bright years, long enough to become a very attractive child and to give a severe wrench to her heart when it left her. This experience seems to have a certain fitness in a life in which every joy was to bring sorrow and every sorrow, by sheer will, was to be turned to joy.

Of Mr. Ware, it is said that this first year " was one of the most active and also, to all human appearance, one of the most successful of his ministry." He put more work into his sermons, gave increased attention to the details of his parish, delivered a course of lectures, and undertook other enterprises, some of which are specified; and, during a temporary absence of Mrs. Ware, wrote her that he had hoped he had turned over a new leaf, " but by foolish degrees, I have got back to all my accustomed careless-ness and waste of powers, and am doing nothing in proportion to what I ought to do."

But man is mortal, and there is a limit to human endurance. Mr. Ware could not lash himself into greater activity; but he was in good condition to be ill. In a journey from North-ampton, he was prostrated by inflammation of the lungs, with hemorrhages, and after several weeks, Mrs. Ware, herself far from well, went to him and finally brought him home. This was the beginning of what became a very regular annual experience. I met a lady who was brought up on the Memoirs of Mary L. Ware, and who briefly put what had impressed her most, in this way: She said, " It seemed as though Mr. Ware was always going off on a journey for his health, and that Mrs. Ware was always going after him to bring him home"; if we remember this statement, and add the fact that these calls came more than once when Mrs. Ware was on the sick list herself, we shall be able greatly to shorten our history.

This was the end of Mr. Ware's parish work. He was nursed through the winter and, in early spring, Mrs. Ware left her baby and took her invalid husband abroad, in pursuit of health, spending a year and a half in England, Holland, Switzerland, and Italy. It was, she afterward said, the most trying period of her life. Mr. Ware alternated between being fairly comfortable and very miserable, so that these Memoirs say "He enjoyed much, but suffered more." Still the travels would be interesting if we had time to follow them.

Near the close of the first year abroad, Mrs. Ware's second child was born in Rome, and, although this was as she would have said, " providential," never was a child less needed in a family. Mrs. Ware had then two babies on her hands, and of these, her invalid husband was the greater care. In the following August, Mrs. Ware arrived in Boston with her double charge, and had the happiness to know that Mr. Ware was somewhat better in health than when he left home, a year and a half before.

His parish, during his absence, had been in the care of a colleague, no other than the Rev. Ralph Waldo Emerson. If you remember the New Year's Eve sermon of Mr. Ware, it will be evident that he must have left behind him a very conservative parish, and you will not be surprised that in about four years, Mr. Emerson found his chains intolerable.

Mr. Ware had been invited to a professorship in the Harvard Divinity School, and it was to this and not to his parish that he returned. For the steady, one might say monotonous, duties of his professorship, Mr. Ware's health was generally sufficient. The lecture room did not exact the several hundred parish calls then demanded by a large city church, nor the exhausting effort which Mr. Ware and Dr. Channing put into the delivery of a sermon; and the lectures, once prepared, could be delivered and redelivered from year to year. Real leisure was impossible to one of Mr. Ware's temperament, but here was a life of comparative leisure; and for Mrs. Ware, who shared all the joys and sorrows of her husband, the twelve years that follow brought a settled existence and very much happiness. Neither her own health nor that of her husband was ever very firm, and there was always a great emptiness in the family purse, but with Mrs. Ware, these were, as with Paul, " light afflictions " which were but for a moment, and she did not let them disturb her happiness.

Impossible as it may seem, they contributed to her happiness. She made them contribute to it. She says in a letter of 1831, " Of my winter's sickness I cannot write; it contained a long life of enjoyment, and what I hoped would be profitable thought and reflection." She repeats this statement to another correspondent, and says, with apparent regret, that the illness did not bring her " to that cheerful willingness to resign my life, after which I strove." You cannot send this woman any trial which she will not welcome, because she wants to be made to want to go to heaven, and she is as yet not quite ready for it.

Mr. Ware has been dangerously ill, and of course she could not spare herself for heaven until he recovered, but this trial did something quite as good for her: " My husband's danger renewed the so oft repeated testimony that strength is ever at hand for those who need it, gave me another exercise of trust in that mighty arm which can save to the uttermost, and in its result is a new cause for gratitude to Him who has so abundantly blessed me all the days of my life." It is good to see what the old-fashioned doctrine that God really is, and is good, did for one who actually believed.

That first baby, whom she left behind when she went abroad with her invalid husband, died in 1831; the mother fainted when the last breath left the little body; but this is the way she writes of it: " I have always looked upon the death of children rather as a subject of joy than sorrow, and have been perplexed at seeing so many, who would bear what seemed to me much harder trials with firmness, so completely overwhelmed by this, as is frequently the case."

After that, one is almost ashamed to mention the trifle that the income of this family was very small. Mr. Ware, after 1834 *Dr.* Ware, held a new professorship, the endowment of which was yet mostly imaginary. The social demands took no account of the family income; the unexpected guest always dropping in; at certain times, it is said, " shoals of visitors "; and the larder always a little scantily furnished. If one wants to know how one ought to live under such circumstances, here is your shining example. " There were no apologies at that table," we are told. " If unexpected guests were not always filled, they were never annoyed, nor suffered to think much about it." " I remember," says a guest,

" the wonder I felt at her humility and dignity in welcoming to her table on some occasion a troop of accidental guests, when she had almost nothing to offer but her hospitality. The absence of all apologies and of all mortification, the ease and cheerfulness of the conversation, which became the only feast, gave me a lesson never forgotten, although never learned."

The problem of dress was as simple to Mrs. Ware as was the entertainment of her guests. " As to her attire," says an intimate friend, " we should say no one thought of it at all, because of its simplicity, and because of her ease of manners and dignity of character. Yet the impression is qualified, though in one view confirmed, by hearing that, in a new place of residence, so plain was her appearance on all occasions, the villagers suspected her of reserving her fine clothes for some better class." There are those who might consider these circumstances, very sore privations. What Mrs. Ware says of them is, " I have not a word of complaint to make. We are far better provided for than is necessary to our happiness." I am persuaded that this is an immensely wholesome example and that more of this kind of woman is needed to mother the children of our generation. In a letter to one of her daughters, she says she has great sympathy with the struggles of young people, that she had struggles too and learned her lessons young, that she found very early in life that her own position was not in the least affected by these externals, " I soon began to look upon my oft-turned dress with something like pride, certainly with great complacency; and to see in that and all other marks of my mother's prudence and consistency, only so many proofs of her dignity and self-respect,— the dignity and self-respect which grew out of her just estimate of the true and the right in herself and in the world."

We have seen enough of this woman to discover that she could not be made unhappy, and also to discover why. It was because her nature was so large and strong and fine. Sometimes she thinks Dr. Ware would be better and happier in a parish, " But I have no care about the future other than that which one must have, — a desire to fulfil the duties which it may bring." Surely that is being,

" Self-poised and independent still
On this world's varying good or ill."

In 1842, Dr. Ware's health became so much

impaired that Mrs. Ware entertains an unful-filled desire. It is to get away from Cambridge, which had become so dear to them all. " I scruple not to say that a ten-foot house, and bread and water diet, with a sense of rest to *him*, would be a luxury." The family removed to Framingham, where Dr. Ware died, a year later. Whatever tribulations might be in store for Mrs. Ware, anxiety on his account was not to be one of them.

Death came on Friday; on Sunday, Mrs. Ware attended church with all her family, and the occasion must have been more trying for the minister who preached to her than for herself. A short service was held that Sunday evening at six, and " Then," she says, " John and I brought dear father's body to Cambridge in our own carriage; we could not feel willing to let stran-gers do anything in connection with him which we could do ourselves." Think of that dark, silent lonely ride from Framingham to Cam-bridge! But here was a woman who did not spare herself, and did not ask what somebody would think of her doings.

After this event, the Memoirs tell us that a gentleman in Milton gave her a very earnest in-vitation to go there and take the instruction of three little children in connection with her own. In this occupation she spent six years of great outward comfort and usefulness. There is much in these years, or in the letters of these years, of great interest and moral beauty. Even with young children to leave, she speaks of death as serenely as she would of going to Boston. "I do not feel that I am essential to my children. I do not feel that I am competent to train them."

Of her last illness, one of her children wrote, "Never did a sick room have less of the odor of sickness than that. It was the brightest spot on earth." "Come with a *smile*," she said to a friend whom she had summoned for a last fare-well, and so went this remarkable and exceptionally noble woman.

III
LYDIA MARIA CHILD

LYDIA MARIA CHILD

In the second quarter of the nineteenth century, few names in American literature were more conspicuous than that of Lydia Maria Child, and among those few, if we except that of Miss Sedgwick, there was certainly no woman's name. Speaking with that studied reserve which became its dignity, the *North American Review* said of her: "We are not sure that any woman of our country could outrank Mrs. Child. This lady has been before the public as an author with much success. And she well deserves it, for in all her works, nothing can be found which does not commend itself by its tone of healthy morality and good sense. Few female writers if any have done more or better things for our literature in the lighter or graver departments."

Mrs. Child began her literary career in 1824 with "Hobomok, a Tale of Early Times," and she closed it with a volume of biography, entitled "Good Wives," in 1871. Between these two dates, covering forty-seven years, her publications extended to more than thirty titles, and

[79]

include stories, poems, biographies, studies in history, in household economics, in politics, and in religion. " Her books," says Col. Higginson, " never seemed to repeat each other and belonged to almost as many different departments as there are volumes "; and while writing so much, he adds, " she wrote better than most of her contemporaries."

If she had not done many things so well, she would still have the distinction of having done several things the first time they were ever done at all. It has been claimed that she edited the first American magazine for children, wrote the first novel of puritan times, published the first American Anti-Slavery book, and compiled the first treatise upon what is now known as " Comparative Religions," a science not then named, but now a department in every school of theology.

Mrs. Child's maiden name was Francis, and under that name she won her first fame. She was born in Medford, Mass., Feb. 11, 1802. Her father, Convers Francis, is said to have been a worthy and substantial citizen, a baker by trade, and the author of the " Medford Crackers," in their day second only in popularity to " Medford Rum." He was a man of strong

LYDIA MARIA CHILD

character, great industry, uncommon love of reading, zealous anti-slavery convictions, generous and hospitable. All these traits were repeated in his famous daughter. It was the custom of Mr. Francis, on the evening before Thanksgiving to gather in his dependents and humble friends to the number of twenty or thirty, and feast them on chicken pie, doughnuts and other edibles, sending them home with provisions for a further festival, including " turnovers " for the children. Col. Higginson, who had the incident from Mrs. Child, intimates that in this experience she may have discovered how much more blessed it is to give than to receive. Certainly, in later life, she believed and practiced this doctrine like a devotee.

Mrs. Child began to climb the hill of knowledge under the instruction of a maiden lady known as " Ma'am Betty," who kept school in her bedroom which was never in order, drank from the nose of her tea-kettle, chewed tobacco and much of it, and was shy to a degree said to have been " supernatural," but she knew the way to the hearts of children, who were very fond of her and regularly carried her a Sunday dinner. After " Ma'am Betty," Mrs. Child attended the public schools in Medford and had a year at a Medford private seminary.

These opportunities for education were cut off at the age of twelve apparently by some change in the family fortunes which compelled the removal of Maria to Norridgewock, Maine, on the borders of the great northern wilderness, where a married sister was living. An influence to which she gave chief credit for her intellectual development and which was not wholly cut off by this removal was that of Convers Francis, her favorite brother, next older than herself, afterward minister in Watertown, and professor in the Divinity School of Harvard University. In later life, Dr. Francis was an encyclopedia of information and scholarship, very liberal in his views for the time. Theodore Parker used to head pages in his journal with, " Questions to ask Dr. Francis."

Dr. Francis began to prepare for college when Mrs. Child was nine years old. Naturally the little girl wanted to read the books which her brother read, and sometimes he seems to have instructed her and sometimes he tantalized her, but always he stimulated her. Years afterward she wrote him gratefully, " To your early influence, by conversation, letters, and example I

owe it that my busy energies took a literary di-
rection at all."

Norridgewock, her home from her twelfth to
her eighteenth year, was and is a very pretty
country village, at that era the residence of some
very cultivated families, but hardly an educational center. As we hear nothing of schools
either there or elsewhere we are led to suppose
that this twelve year old girl had finished her education. If she lacked opportunities for culture,
she carried with her a desire for it, which is half
the battle, and she had the intellectual stimulus of
letters from her brother then in college, who
seems to have presided over her reading. What
we know of her life at this period is told in her
letters to this brother.

The first of these letters which the editors let
us see was written at the age of fifteen. " I
have," she says, " been busily engaged reading
Paradise Lost. Homer hurried me along with
rapid impetuosity; every passion that he portrayed I felt; I loved, hated, and resented just
as he inspired me. But when I read Milton I
felt elevated ' above this visible, diurnal sphere.'
I could not but admire such astonishing grand-
eur of description, such heavenly sublimity of

style.   Much as I admire Milton, I must confess that Homer is a much greater favorite."

It is not strange that a studious brother in college would take interest in a sister who at the age of fifteen could write him with so much intelligence and enthusiasm of her reading. The next letter is two years later when she has been reading Scott.   She likes Meg Merrilies, Diana Vernon, Annot Lyle, and Helen Mac Gregor.   She hopes she may yet read Virgil in his own tongue, and adds, "I usually spend an hour after I retire for the night in reading Gibbon's Roman Empire.   The pomp of his style at first displeased me, but I think him an able historian."

This is from a girl of seventeen living on the edge of the northern wilderness, and she is also reading Shakspere.   "What a vigorous grasp of intellect," she says, "what a glow of imagination he must have possessed, but when his fancy drops a little, how apt he is to make low attempts at wit, and introduce a forced play upon words." She is also reading the Spectator, and does not think Addison so good a writer as Johnson, though a more polished one.

What she was doing with her ever busy hands during this period we are not told, but her intellectual life ran on in these channels until she reaches the age of eighteen, when she is engaged to teach a school in Gardiner, Maine, an event which makes her very happy. " I cannot talk about books," she writes, " nor anything else until I tell you the good news, that I leave Norridgewock as soon as the travelling is tolerable and take a school in Gardiner." It is the terrible month of March, for country roads in the far north, " the saddest of the year." She wishes her brother were as happy as she is, though, " All I expect is that, if I am industrious and prudent, I shall be independent."

At the conclusion of her school, she took up her residence with her brother in Watertown, Mass., where one year before, he had been settled as minister of the first parish. Here a new career opened before her. Whittier says that in her Norridgewock period, when she first read Waverly at the house of her physician, she laid down the book in great excitement, exclaiming, " Why cannot I write a novel?" Apparently, she did not undertake the enterprise for two years or more. In 1824, one Sunday after morning service, in her brother's study, she read an article in the *North American Review*, in which it was pointed out that there were great possibilities of romance in early American history. Before the afternoon service, she had written the first chapter of a novel which was published anonymously the same year, under the title of " Hobomok: a Tale of Early Times."

A search through half a dozen Antique Book stores in Boston for a copy of this timid literary venture I have found to be fruitless, except for the information that there is sometimes a stray copy in stock, and that its present value is about three dollars. It is sufficient distinction that it was the first attempt to extract a romantic element from early New England history. Its reception by the public was flattering to a young author. The Boston Athenæum sent her a ticket granting the privileges of its library. So great and perhaps unexpected had been its success that for several years, Mrs. Child's books bore the signature, " By the author of Hobomok." Even " The Frugal Housewife " was " By the author of Hobomok."

In 1825, the author of Hobomok published her second novel, entitled, " The Rebels: a Tale of the Revolution." It is a volume of about 300 pages, and is still very readable. It ran rapidly through several editions, and very much increased the reputation of the author of Hobomok. The work contains an imaginary speech of James Otis, in which it is said, " England might as well dam up the Nile with bulrushes as to fetter the step of Freedom, more proud and firm in this youthful land than where she treads the sequestered glens of Scotland or couches herself among the magnificent mountains of Switzerland." This supposed speech of Otis soon found its way into the School Readers of the day, as a genuine utterance of the Revolutionary patriot, and as such Col. Higginson says he memorized and declaimed it, in his youth.

This literary success was achieved at the age of twenty-three, and the same year Miss Francis opened a private school in Watertown, which she continued three years, until her marriage gave her other occupations. In 1826, she started *The Juvenile Miscellany*, as already mentioned, said to be the first magazine expressly for children, in this country. In it, first appeared many of her charming stories afterward gathered up in little volumes entitled, " Flowers for Children."

In 1828, she was married to Mr. David Lee Child, then 34 years of age, eight years older than herself. Whittier describes him as a young and able lawyer, a member of the Massachusetts legislature, and editor of the *Massachusetts*

Journal. Mr. Child graduated at Harvard in 1817 in the class with George Bancroft, Caleb Cushing, George B. Emerson, and Samuel J. May. Between 1818 and 1824, he was in our diplomatic service abroad under Hon. Alexander Everett, at that time, Chargé d'Affaires in the Netherlands. On his return to America, Mr. Child studied law in Watertown where, at the house of a mutual friend, he met Miss Lydia Maria Francis. She herself reports this interesting event under date of Dec. 2, 1824. " Mr. Child dined with us in Watertown. He possesses the rich fund of an intelligent traveller, without the slightest tinge of a traveller's vanity. Spoke of the tardy improvement of the useful arts in Spain and Italy." Nearly two months pass, when we have this record: " Jan. 26, 1825. Saw Mr. Child at Mr. Curtis's. He is the most gallant man that has lived since the sixteenth century and needs nothing but helmet, shield, and chain-armor to make him a complete knight of chivalry." Not all the meetings are recorded, for, some weeks later, " March 3," we have this entry, " One among the many delightful evenings spent with Mr. Child. I do not know which to admire most, the vigor of his understanding or the ready sparkle of his wit."

There can be no doubt that she thoroughly enjoyed these interviews, and we shall have to discount the statement of any observer who gathered a different impression. Mr. George Ticknor Curtis, at whose home some of these interviews took place, was a boy of twelve, and may have taken the play of wit between the parties too seriously. He says, " At first Miss Francis did not like Mr. Child. Their intercourse was mostly banter and mutual criticism. Observers said, ' Those two people will end in marrying.' Miss Francis was not a beautiful girl in the ordinary sense, but her complexion was good, her eyes were bright, her mouth expressive and her teeth fine. She had a great deal of wit, liked to use it, and did use it upon Mr. Child who was a frequent visitor; but her deportment was always maidenly and lady-like."

The engagement happened in this wise. Mr. Child had been admitted to the bar and had opened an office in Boston. One evening about nine o'clock he rode out to Watertown on horseback and called at the Curtises' where Miss Francis then was. "My mother, who believed the denouement had come," says Mr. Curtis, " retired to her chamber. Mr. Child pressed his suit earnestly. Ten o'clock came, then eleven, then twelve. The horse grew impatient and Mr. Child went out once or twice to pacify him, and returned. At last, just as the clock was striking one, he went. Miss Francis rushed into my mother's room and told her she was engaged to Mr. Child."

There are indications in this communication that Mr. Curtis did not himself greatly admire Mr. Child and would not have married him, but he concedes that, "Beyond all doubt, Mrs. Child was perfectly happy in her relations with him, through their long life." After their marriage, he says, they went to housekeeping in a "very small house in Boston," where Mr. Curtis, then a youth of sixteen, visited them and partook of a simple, frugal dinner which the lady cooked and served with her own hands, and to which Mr. Child returned from his office, "cheery and breezy," and we may hope the vivacity of the host may have made up for the frugality of the entertainment.

In "Letters from New York," written to the Boston *Courier*, she speaks tenderly of her Boston home which she calls "Cottage Place" and declares it the dearest spot on earth. I assume it was this "very small house" where she began her married life, where she dined the fastidious

Mr. Curtis, and where she seems to have spent eight or nine happy years. Her marriage brought her great happiness. A friend says, " The domestic happiness of Mr. and Mrs. Child seemed to me perfect. Their sympathies, their admiration of all things good, and their hearty hatred of all things mean and evil, were in entire unison. Mr. Child shared his wife's enthusiasms and was very proud of her. Their affection, never paraded, was always manifest." After Mr. Child's death, Mrs. Child said, " I believe a future life would be of small value to me, if I were not united to him."

Mr. Child was a man of fine intellect, with studious tastes and habits, but there is too much reason to believe that his genius did not lie in the management of practical life. Details of business were apparently out of his sphere. " It was like cutting stones with a razor," says one who knew him. " He was a visionary," says another, " who always saw a pot of gold at the foot of the rainbow." This was a kind of defect which, though it cost her dear, Mrs. Child, of all persons, could most easily forgive. One great success he achieved: that was in winning and keeping the heart of Mrs. Child. Their married life seems to have been one long honeymoon. " I always depended," she says, " upon his richly stored mind, which was able and ready to furnish needed information on any subject. He was my walking dictionary of many languages, and my universal encyclopedia. In his old age, he was as affectionate and devoted as when the lover of my youth; nay, he manifested even more tenderness. He was often singing,

> ' There's nothing half so sweet in life
>   As love's *old* dream.'

Very often, when he passed me, he would lay his hand softly on my head and murmur ' Carum Caput.' . . . He never would see anything but the bright side of my character. He always insisted upon thinking that whatever I said was the wisest and whatever I did was the best."

In the anti-slavery conflict, Mr. Child's name was among the earliest, and at the beginning of the controversy, few were more prominent. In 1832, he published in Boston a series of articles upon slavery and the slave-trade; in 1836, another series upon the same subject, in Philadelphia; in 1837, an elaborate memoir upon the subject for an anti-slavery society in France, and an able article in a *London Review.* It is said that the speeches of John Quincy Adams in Congress were greatly indebted to the writings of Mr. Child, both for facts and arguments.

Such, briefly, is the man with whom Mrs. Child is to spend forty-five years of her useful and happy life. In 1829, the year after her marriage, she put her twelve months of experience and reflection into a book entitled, " The Frugal Housewife." " No false pride," she says, " or foolish ambition to appear as well as others, should induce a person to live a cent beyond the income of which he is assured." " We shall never be free from embarrassment until we cease to be ashamed of industry and economy." " The earlier children are taught to turn their faculties to some account the better for them and for their parents." " A child of six years is old enough to be made useful and should be taught to consider every day lost in which some little thing has not been done to assist others." We are told that a child can be taught to braid straw for his hats or to make feather fans; the objection to which would be that a modern mother would not let a child wear that kind of hat nor carry the fan.

The following will be interesting if not valuable: " Cheap as stockings are, it is good economy to knit them; knit hose wear twice as long as woven; and they can be done at odd moments of time which would not be otherwise employed." What an age that must have been when one had time enough and to spare! Other suggestions are quite as curious. The book is " dedicated to those who are not ashamed of economy." " The writer," she says, " has no apology to offer for this little book of economical hints, except her deep conviction that such a book is needed. In this case, renown is out of the question; and ridicule is a matter of indifference."

Goethe made poems of his chagrins; Mrs. Child in this instance utilized her privations and forced economies to make a book; and a wonderfully successful book it was. She was not wrong in supposing it would meet a want. During the next seven years, it went through twenty editions, or three editions a year; in 1855, it had reached its thirty-third edition, averaging little short of one edition a year for thirty-six years. Surely this was a result which made a year of economical living in a " very small house " worth while.

" The Frugal Housewife " was a true

" mother's book," although another and later volume was so named. " The Mother's Book " was nearly as successful as " The Frugal Housewife," and went through eight American editions, twelve English, and one German. The success of these books gave Mrs. Child a good income, and she hardly needed to be the " frugal housewife " she had been before.

A check soon came to her prosperity. In 1831, she met Garrison and, being inflammable, caught fire from his anti-slavery zeal, and became one of his earliest and staunchest disciples. The free use of the Athenæum library which had been graciously extended to her ten years before, now enabled her to study the subject of slavery in all its aspects, historical, legal, theoretical, and practical and, in 1833, she embodied the results of her investigations in a book entitled, " An Appeal in behalf of the class of Americans called Africans." The material is chiefly drawn from Southern sources, the statute books of Southern states, the columns of Southern newspapers, and the statements and opinions of Southern public men. It is an effective book to read even now when one is in a mood to rose-color the old-time plantation life and doubtful whether anything could be worse than the present condition of the negro in the South.

The book had two kinds of effect. It brought upon Mrs. Child the incontinent wrath of all persons who, for any reason, thought that the only thing to do with slavery was to let it alone. " A lawyer, afterward attorney-general," a description that fits Caleb Cushing, is said to have used tongs to throw the obnoxious book out of the window; the Athenæum withdrew from Mrs. Child the privileges of its library; former friends dropped her acquaintance; Boston society shut its doors upon her; the sale of her books fell off; subscriptions to her *Juvenile Miscellany* were discontinued; and the magazine died after a successful life of eight years; and Mrs. Child found that she had ventured upon a costly experiment. This consequence she had anticipated and it had for her no terrors. " I am fully aware," she says in her preface, " of the unpopularity of the task I have undertaken; but though I expect ridicule, I do not fear it. . . . Should it be the means of advancing even one single hour the inevitable progress of truth and justice, I would not exchange the consciousness for all Rothschild's wealth or Sir Walter's fame."

Of course a book of such evident significance

and power would have had another effect; by his own acknowledgement, it brought Dr. Channing into the anti-slavery crusade, and he published a book upon slavery in 1835; it led Dr. John G. Palfry, who had inherited a plantation in Louisiana, to emancipate his slaves; and, as he has more than once said, it changed the course of Col. T. W. Higginson's life and made him an abolitionist. "As it was the first anti-slavery work ever printed in America in book form, so," says Col. Higginson, " I have always thought it the ablest." Whittier says, " It is no exaggeration to say that no man or woman at that period rendered more substantial service to the cause of freedom, or made such a ' great renunciation ' in doing it."

Turning from the real world, which was becoming too hard for her, Mrs. Child took refuge in dreamland and wrote " Philothea: a story of Ancient Greece," published in 1835. Critics have objected that this delightful romance is not an exact reproduction of Greek life, but is Hamlet a reproduction of anything that ever happened in Denmark, or Browning's Saul of anything that could have happened in Judea, a thousand years before Christ? To Lowell, Mrs. Child was and remained " Philothea."

Higginson says that the lines in which Lowell describes her in the "Fable for Critics," are the one passage of pure poetry it contains, and at the same time the most charming sketch ever made of Mrs. Child.

" There comes Philothea, her face all aglow;
She has just been dividing some poor creature's
    woe,
And can't tell which pleases her most — to re-
    lieve
His want, or his story to hear and believe.
No doubt against many deep griefs she prevails,
For her ear is the refuge of destitute tales;
She knows well that silence is sorrow's best food,
And that talking draws off from the heart its bad
    blood."

In 1836, Mr. Child went abroad to study the Beet Sugar industry in France, Holland, and Germany and, after an absence of a year and a half, returned to engage in Beet Sugar Farming at Northampton, Mass. He received a silver medal for raw and refined sugar at the Exhibition of the Massachusetts Charitable Mechanics Association in 1839, and a premium of $100 from the Massachusetts Agricultural society the same year. He published a well written and edifying book upon " Beet Sugar," giving the results of his investigations and experiments. It was an enterprise of great promise, but has taken half a century, in this country, to become a profitable industry.

Mrs. Child's letters from 1838 to 1841 are dated from Northampton, where she is assisting to work out the " Beet Sugar " experiment. It would have been a rather grinding experience to any one with less cheerfulness than Mrs. Child. She writes, June 9, 1838, " A month elapsed before I stepped into the woods which were all around me blooming with flowers. I did not go to Mr. Dwight's ordination, nor have I yet been to meeting. He has been to see me however, and though I left my work in the midst and sat down with a dirty gown and hands somewhat grimmed, we were high in the blue in fifteen minutes." Mr. Dwight was Rev. John S. Dwight, Brook Farmer, and editor of *Dwight's Journal of Music.*

Half of her published letters are addressed to Mr. or Mrs. Francis G. Shaw, parents of Col. Robert G. Shaw. Here is one in 1840, to Mr. Shaw, after she had made a trip to Boston. It will be interesting as presenting a new aspect of Mrs. Child's nature: " The only thing, except meeting dear friends, that attracted me to Boston was the exhibition of statuary. . . . I am ashamed to say how deeply I am charmed with sculpture: ashamed because it seems like affectation in one who has had such limited opportunity to become acquainted with the arts. I have a little figure of a caryatid which acts upon my spirit like a magician's spell. . . . Many a time this hard summer, I have laid down my dish-cloth or broom and gone to refresh my spirit by gazing on it a few minutes. It speaks to me. It says glorious things. In summer I place flowers before it; and I have laid a garland of acorns and amaranths at its feet. I do love every little bit of real sculpture."

Her other artistic passion was music, quite out of her reach at this period; but happily, she loved birds and flowers, both of which a Beet Sugar Farm in the Connecticut Valley made possible. A family of swallows made their nest in her woodshed, husband and wife dividing the labors of construction, nursing, and even of incubation, though the male bird did not have the same skill and grace as the lady, in placing his feet and wings. Mrs. Child gives a pretty account of this incident in a letter to one of her little friends, and says, " It seems as if I could watch them forever."

Later, in one of her letters to the Boston *Courier*, she gives a more complete account of the episode. Her observations convinced her that birds have to be taught to fly, as a child is taught to walk.

When birds and flowers went, she had the autumn foliage, and she managed to say a new thing about it: it is " color taking its fond and bright farewell of form — like the imagination giving a deeper, richer, and warmer glow to old familiar truths before the winter of rationalism comes and places trunk and branches in naked outline against the cold, clear sky."

Whether she had been living hitherto in a " rent " we are not told, but in a letter of February 8, 1841, she informs us that she is about to move to a farm on which " is a sort of a shanty with two rooms and a garret. We expect to whitewash it, build a new woodshed, and live there next year. I shall keep no help, and there will be room for David and me. I intend to half bury it in flowers."

There is nothing fascinating in sordid details, but Mrs. Child in the midst of sordid details, is glorious. A month before this last letter, her brother, Prof. Francis, had written her apparently wishing her more congenial circumstances; we have only her reply, from which it appears her father is under her care. She declines her brother's sympathy, and wonders that he can suppose " the deadening drudgery of the world " can imprison a soul in its caverns. " It is not merely an eloquent phrase," she says, " but a distinct truth that the outward has no power over us but that which we voluntarily give it. It is not I who drudge; it is merely the case that contains me. I defy all the powers of earth and hell to make me scour floors and feed pigs, if I choose meanwhile to be off conversing with angels. . . . If I can in quietude and cheerfulness forego my own pleasures and relinquish my tastes, to administer to my father's daily comfort, I seem to those who live in shadows to be cooking food and mixing medicines, but I am in fact making divine works of art which will reveal to me their fair proportions in the far eternity." Besides this consolation, she says, " Another means of keeping my soul fresh is my intense love of nature. Another help, perhaps stronger than either of the two, is domestic love."

Her Northampton life was nearer an end than she supposed when she wrote these letters; she did not spend the next year in the little

farm house with "two rooms and a garret";
on May 27th, she dates a letter from New York
city, where she has gone reluctantly to edit the
Anti-Slavery Standard. She had been translated from the sphere of "cooking food and
mixing medicines" to congenial literary occupations; she had, let us hope, a salary sufficient
for her urgent necessities; her home was in the
family of the eminent Quaker philanthropist,
Isaac T. Hopper, who received her as a daughter, and whose kindness she repaid by writing
his biography. However the venture might
come out, we would think her life could not well
be harder or less attractive than it had been,
drudging in a dilapidated farm house, and we
are glad she is well out of it. Strange to say,
she did not take our view of the situation. We
have already seen how independent she was of
external circumstances. In a letter referred
to, dated May 27, she chides a friend for
writing accounts of her outward life: "What
do I care whether you live in one room or six?
I want to know what your spirit is doing.
What are you thinking, feeling, and reading?
. . . My task here is irksome enough.
Your father will tell you that it was not zeal
for the cause, but love for my husband, which

brought me hither. But since it was necessary for me to leave home to be earning somewhat, I am thankful that my work is for the anti-slavery cause. I have agreed to stay one year. I hope I shall then be able to return to my husband and rural home, which is humble enough, yet very satisfactory to me. Should the *Standard* be continued, and my editing generally desired, perhaps I could make an arrangement to send articles from Northampton. 'At all events, I trust the weary separation from my husband is not to last more than a year. If I am to be away from him, I could not be more happily situated than in Friend Hopper's family. They treat me the same as a daughter and a sister."

The *Anti-Slavery Standard* was a new enterprise; its editorship was offered to Mr. and Mrs. Childs jointly; Col. Higginson says that Mr. Child declined because of ill health; another authority, that he was still infatuated with his Beet Sugar, of which Mrs. Child had had more than enough; it appears from her letter that neither of them dreamed of abandoning the Sugar industry; if the enterprise was folly, they were happily united in the folly.

However, of the two, the *Anti-Slavery*

Standard was the more successful enterprise, and at the end of the two years, Mr. Child closed out his Beet Sugar business and joined Mrs. Child in editing the paper. Mrs. Child edited the *Standard* eight years, six of which were in conjunction with Mr. Child. They were successful editors; they gave the *Standard* a high literary character, and made it acceptable to people of taste and culture who, whatever their sympathy with anti-slavery, were often repelled by the unpolished manners of Mr. Garrison's paper, *The Liberator*.

Something of her life outside the *Standard* office, something of the things she saw and heard and enjoyed, during these eight years, can be gathered from her occasional letters to the Boston *Courier*. They are interesting still; they will always be of interest to one who cares to know old New York, as it was sixty years ago, or from 1840 onward. That they were appreciated then is evident from the fact that, collected and published in two volumes in 1844, eleven editions were called for during the next eight years. Col. Higginson considers these eight years in New York the most interesting and satisfactory of Mrs. Child's life.

Though we have room for few incidents of this

period, there is one too charming to be omitted. A friend went to a flower merchant on Broadway to buy a bunch of violets for Mrs. Child's birthday. Incidentally, the lady mentioned Mrs. Child; she may have ordered the flowers sent to her house. When the lady came to pay for them, the florist said, " I cannot take pay for flowers intended for her. She is a stranger to me, but she has given my wife and children so many flowers in her writings, that I will never take money of her." Another pretty incident is this: an unknown friend or admirer always sent Mrs. Child the earliest wild flowers of spring and the latest in autumn.

I have said that one of her passions was music, which happily she now has opportunities to gratify. " As for amusements," she says, " music is the only thing that excites me. . . . I have a chronic insanity with regard to music. It is the only Pegasus which now carries me far up into the blue. Thank God for this blessing of mine." I should be glad if I had room for her account of an evening under the weird spell of Ole Bull. Her moral sense was keener than her æsthetic, but her æsthetic sense was for keener than that of the average mortal. Sometimes she felt, as Paul would have said,

" in a strait betwixt two "; in 1847 she writes
Mr. Francis G. Shaw: " I am now wholly in the
dispensation of art, and therefore theologians
and reformers jar upon me." Reformer as she
was and will be remembered, she was easily
drawn into the dispensation of art; and nature
was always with her, so much so that Col. Higginson says, " She always seemed to be talking
radicalism in a greenhouse."

Mr. and Mrs. Child retired from the *Standard* in 1849. Her next letters are dated from
Newton, Mass. Her father was living upon a
small place — a house and garden — in the
neighboring town of Wayland, beautifully
situated, facing Sudbury Hill, with the broad
expanse of the river meadows between.
Thither Mrs. Child went to take care of him
from 1852 to 1856, when he died, leaving the
charming little home to her. There are many
traditions of her mode of life in Wayland, but
her own account is the best: " In 1852, we made
our humble home in Wayland, Mass., where we
spent twenty-two pleasant years, entirely alone,
without any domestic, mutually serving each
other and depending upon each other for intellectual companionship." If the memory of
Wayland people is correct, Mr. Child was not

with her much during the four years that her
father lived.   Her father was old and feeble and
Mr. Child had not the serene patience of his
wife.   Life ran more easily when Mr. Child was
away.   Whatever other period in the life of
Mrs. Child may have been the most satisfactory,
this must have been the most trying.

Under date of March 23, 1856, happily the
last year of this sort of widowhood, she writes:
" This winter has been the loneliest of my life.
If you knew my situation you would pronounce
it unendurable.   I should have thought so myself if I had had a foreshadowing of it a few
years ago.   But the human mind can get accli-
mated to anything.   What with constant occupation and a happy consciousness of sustaining
and cheering my poor old father in his descent
to the grave, I am almost always in a state of
serene contentment.   In summer, my once ex-
travagant love of beauty satisfies itself in
watching the birds, the insects, and the flowers in
my little patch of a garden." She has no
room for her vases, engravings, and other
pretty things; she keeps them in a chest, and
she says. " when birds and flowers are gone, I
sometimes take them out as a child does its

playthings, and sit down in the sunshine with them, dreaming over them."

We need not think of her spending much time dreaming over her little hoard of artistic treasures. Her real business in this world is writing the history of all religions, or "The Progress of Religious Ideas in Successive Ages." It was a work begun in New York, as early as 1848, finished in Wayland in 1855, published in three large octavo volumes and, whatever its merits or success, was the greatest literary labor of her life.

Under date of July 14, 1848, she writes to Dr. Francis: " My book gets slowly on. . . . I am going to tell the plain, unvarnished truth, as clearly as I can understand it, and let Christians and Infidels, Orthodox and Unitarians, Catholics, Protestants, and Swedenborgians growl as they like. They will growl if they notice it at all: for each will want his own theory favored, and the only thing I have conscientiously aimed at is not to favor any theory at all." She may have failed in scientific method; but here is a scientific spirit. " In her religious speculations," says Whittier, " Mrs. Child moved in the very van." In Wayland, she considered herself a parishioner of Dr. Edmund

H. Sears, whom she calls, "our minister," but she was somewhat in advance of Dr. Sears. Her opinions were much nearer akin to those of Theodore Parker. Only a Unitarian of that type could perhaps at this early period have conceived the history of religion as an evolution of one and the same spiritual element "through successive ages."

She had not much time to dream over her chest of artistic treasures when the assault of Preston S. Brooks upon Senator Sumner called her to battle of such force and point that Dr. William H. Furness said, it was worth having Sumner's head broken.

When death released her from the care of her father, she took "Bleeding Kansas" under her charge. She writes letters to the newspapers; she sits up till eleven o'clock, "stitching as fast as my fingers could go," making garments for the Kansas immigrants; she "stirs up the Wayland women to make garments for Kansas"; she sends off Mr. Child to make speeches for Kansas; and then she writes him in this manner: "How melancholy I felt when you went off in the morning darkness. It seemed as if everything about me was tumbling down; as if I were never to have a nest and a mate any more." Surely the rest of this letter was not written for us to read: " Good, kind, magnanimous soul, how I love you. How I long to say over the old prayer again every night. It almost made me cry to see how carefully you had arranged everything for my comfort before you went; so much kindling stuff split up and the bricks piled up to protect my flowers." Here is love in a cottage. This life is not all prosaic.

Old anti-slavery friends came to see her and among them Charles Sumner, in 1857, spent a couple of hours with her, and left his photograph; she met Henry Wilson at the anti-slavery fair and talked with him an " hour or so." Whittier says, " Men like Charles Sumner, Henry Wilson, Salmon P. Chase, and Governor Andrew availed themselves of her foresight and sound judgment of men and measures."

When John Brown was wounded and taken prisoner at Harper's Ferry, nothing was more in character for Mrs. Child than to offer her services as his nurse. She wrote him under cover of a letter to Gov. Wise, of Virginia. The arrival of Mrs. Brown, made Mrs. Child's attendance unnecessary, but the incident led to a lively correspondence between Mrs. Child and

Gov. Wise, in which Mrs. Senator Mason, of Virginia, joined. Neither of her distinguished correspondents possessed the literary skill of Mrs. Child. The entire correspondence was collected in a pamphlet of which 300,000 copies were sold. On a visit to Whittier at Amesbury, a delegation from a Republican political meeting called upon her, saying they wanted to see the woman who " poured hot shot into Gov. Wise."

In 1863, after saying that she is " childish enough to talk to the picture of a baby that is being washed," she writes her friend, Mrs. Shaw, " But you must not suppose that I live for amusement. On the contrary I work like a beaver the whole time. Just now I am making a hood for a poor neighbor; last week I was making flannels for the hospital; odd minutes are filled up ravelling lint; every string that I can get sight of I pull for poor Sambo. I write to the *Tribune* about him; I write to the *Transcript* about him; I write to private individuals about him; and I write to the President and members of Congress about him; I write to Western Virginia and Missouri about him; and I get the articles published too. This shows what progress the cause of freedom is making."

Not everything went to her mind however. If we think there has been a falling from grace in the public life of our generation, it may do us good to read what she says in 1863: "This war has furnished many instances of individual nobility, but our national record is mean."

In 1864, she published "Looking Toward Sunset," a book designed to "present old people with something wholly cheerful." The entire edition was exhausted during the holiday season; 4,000 copies were sold and more called for. All her profits on the book, she devoted to the freedmen, sending $400 as a first instalment. Not only that, but she prepared a volume called "The Freedman's Book," which she printed at an expense of $600, and distributed among the freedmen 1200 copies at her own cost. She once sent Wendell Phillips a check of $100 for the freedmen, and when he protested that it was more than she could afford, she consented to "think it over." The next day, she made her contribution $200. She contributed $20 a year to the American Missionary Association toward the support of a teacher for the freedmen, and $50 a year to the Anti-Slavery Society. A lady wished, through Mr. Phillips, to give Mrs. Child several thousand dollars for her comfort. Mrs. Child declined the favor, but was persuaded to accept it, and then scrupulously gave away the entire income in charity. It is evident she might have made herself very comfortable, if it had not given her so much more pleasure to make someone else comfortable.

Her dress, as neat and clean as that of a Quakeress, was quite as plain and far from the latest style. A stranger meeting her in a stage coach mistook her for a servant until she began to talk. "Who is that woman who dresses like a peasant, and speaks like a scholar?" he asked on leaving the coach. Naturally, it was thought Mrs. Child did not know how to dress, or, more likely, did not care for pretty things. "You accuse me," she writes to Miss Lucy Osgood, "you accuse me of being indifferent to externals, whereas the common charge is that I think too much of beauty, and say too much about it. I myself think it one of my greatest weaknesses. A handsome man, woman or child can always make a pack-horse of me. My next neighbor's little boy has me completely under his thumb, merely by virtue of his beautiful eyes and sweet voice." There was one before her of whom it was said, "He denied himself, and took up his cross." It was also said of him, " Though he was rich, yet for our sakes he became poor." He never had a truer disciple than Mrs. Child.

Not that she ever talked of " crosses." " But why use the word sacrifice? " she asks. " I never was conscious of any sacrifice." What she gained in moral discipline or a new life, she says, was always worth more than the cost. She used an envelope twice, Wendell Phillips says; she never used a whole sheet of paper when half of one would do; she outdid poverty in her economies, and then gave money as if she had thousands. " I seldom have a passing wish for enlarging my income except for the sake of doing more for others. My wants are very few and simple."

In 1867, Mrs. Child published " A Romance of the Republic," a pathetic story, but fascinating, and admirably written; in 1878, appeared a book of choice selections, entitled, " Aspirations of the World "; and in 1871, a volume of short biographies, entitled " Good Wives," and dedicated, to Mr. Child: " To my husband, this book is affectionately inscribed, by one who, through every vicissitude, has found in his kindness and worth, her purest happiness and most constant incentive to duty."

Mr. Child died in 1874 at the age of eighty, and Mrs. Child followed him in 1880, at the age of seventy-eight. After her death, a small volume of her letters was published, of which the reader will wish there were more. Less than a month before her death, she wrote to a friend a list of benevolent enterprises she has in mind and says, " Oh, it is such a luxury to be able to give without being afraid. I try not to be Quixotic, but I want to rain down blessings on all the world, in token of thankfulness for the blessings that have been rained down upon me."

It is too late to make amends for omissions in this paper, but it would be unjust to Mrs. Child to forget her life-long devotion to the interests of her own sex. In 1832, a year before her " Appeal in behalf of that class of Americans called Africans,"— eleven years before the appearance of Margaret Fuller's " Woman in the Nineteenth Century," Mrs. Child published " A History of the Condition of Women in all ages and nations," showing her disposition to begin every inquiry with a survey of the facts, and also that the " woman question " was the first to awaken her interest. Her greatest contribution to the advancement of women was

herself; that is, her own achievements. To the
same purpose were her biographies of famous
women: " Memoirs of Mme. de Stael and Mme.
Roland " in 1847, and sketches of " Good
Wives " in 1871. Whittier says, she always believed in woman's right to the ballot, as certainly he did, calling it " the greatest social reform
of the age." In one letter to Senator Sumner,
she directly argues the question: " I reduce the
argument," she says, " to very simple elements.
I pay taxes for property of my own earning,
and I do not believe in ' taxation without rep-
resentation.' " Again: " I am a human being
and every human being has a right to a voice in
the laws which claim authority to tax him, to
imprison him, or to *hang* him."

A light humor illuminates this argument.
Humor was one of her saving qualities which,
as Whittier says, " kept her philanthropy free
from any taint of fanaticism." It contributed
greatly to her cheerfulness. Of her fame, she
says playfully: " In a literary point of view I
know I have only a local reputation, done in
water colors."

Could anything have been better said than
this of the New England April or even May:
" What a misnomer in our climate to call this

season Spring, very much like calling Calvinism religion." Nothing could have been keener than certain points scored in her reply to Mrs. Senator Mason. Mrs. Mason, remembering with approving conscience her own ministries in the slave cabins caring for poor mothers with young babies, asks Mrs. Child, in triumph, if she goes among the poor to render such services. Mrs. Child replies that she has never known mothers under such circumstances to be neglected, " and here at the North," said she, " after we have helped the mothers, we do not sell the babies." After Gen. Grant's election to the Presidency, a procession with a band from Boston, marched to her house and gave her a serenade. She says that she joined in the hurrahs " like the strong-minded woman that I am. The fact is, I forgot half the time whether I belonged to the stronger or weaker sex." Whether she belonged to the stronger or weaker sex, is still something of a problem. Sensible men would be willing to receive her, should women ever refuse to acknowledge her.

Wendell Phillips paid her an appreciative tribute; at her funeral. " There were," he said, " all the charms and graceful elements which we call feminine, united with a masculine grasp and vigor; sound judgment and great breadth; large common sense and capacity for everyday usefulness, endurance, foresight, strength, and skill." The address is given in full in the volume of "Letters." There is also a fine poem by Whittier for the same occasion:

" Than thine was never turned a fonder heart
    To nature and to art;

Yet loving beauty, thou couldst pass it by,
    And for the poor deny
Thyself . . ."

The volume contains a poetical tribute of an earlier date, by Eliza Scudder, of which Mrs. Child said, " I never was so touched and pleased by any tribute in my life. I cried over the verses and I smiled over them." I will close this paper with Miss Scudder's last stanza:

" So apt to know, so wise to guide,
    So tender to redress,—
  O, friend with whom such charms abide,
    How can I love thee less? "

IV
DOROTHEA LYNDE DIX

DOROTHEA LYNDE DIX

The career of Dorothy Dix is a romance of philanthropy which the world can ill afford to forget. It has been said of her, and it is still said, that she was " the most useful and distinguished woman America has yet produced." It is the opinion of Mr. Tiffany, her biographer, that as the founder of institutions of mercy, she " has simply no peer in the annals of Protestantism." To find her parallel one must go to the calendar of the Catholic saints, — St. Theresa, of Spain, or Santa Chiara, of Assisi. " Why then," he asks, do the " majority of the present generation know little or nothing of so remarkable a story ! " Till his biography appeared, it might have been answered that the story had never been told; now, we should have to say that, with a thousand demands upon our time, it has not been read.

Dorothea Lynde Dix — born February 11, 1802 — was the daughter of Joseph Dix and granddaughter of the more eminent Dr. Elijah Dix, of Worcester, later of Boston, Mass. Dr.

Dix was born in Watertown, Mass., in 1747. At the age of seventeen, he became the office boy of Dr. John Green, an eminent physician in Worcester, Mass., and later, a student of medicine. After five years, in 1770, he began to practice as physician and surgeon in Worcester where he formed a partnership with Dr. Sylvester Gardner. It must have been a favorable time for young doctors since in 1771, a year after he began to practice, he married Dorothy Lynde, of Charlestown, Mass., for whom her little granddaughter was named. Mrs. Dix seems to have been a woman of great decision of character, and no less precision of thought and action, two traits which reappeared conspicuously in our great philanthropist.

Certain qualities of Dr. Dix are also said to have reappeared in his granddaughter. He was self-reliant, aggressive, uncompromising, public-spirited, and sturdily honest. To his enterprise, Worcester owed its first shade trees, planted by him, when shade trees were considered great folly, and also the Boston and Worcester turnpike, when mud roads were thought to be divinely appointed thoroughfares. His integrity is shown by an incident

DOROTHEA LYNDE DIX

which also throws light upon the conditions of
a troubled period. His partner, Dr. Gardner,
made the grave mistake of taking the royal
side in the controversies that preceded the Revolution, and Worcester became as hot for him as
Richmond or Charleston was for a Union man
in 1861. Dr. Gardner disappeared, leaving
his effects behind him. After the war, Dr. Dix
made a voyage to England and honorably settled accounts with his former partner.

It was like the enterprising Dr. Dix that he
turned this creditable act to his financial advantage. On his return to America he brought
with him a stock of medical books, surgical in-
struments, and chemical apparatus, and became
a dealer in physician's supplies, while continu-
ing the practice of his profession. His business prospering, in 1795 he removed to Boston
for a larger field, where he opened a drug store
near Faneuil Hall and established chemical
works in South Boston. Successful as physician, druggist and manufacturer, he soon had
money to invest. Maine, with its timber lands,
was the Eldorado of that era, and Dr. Dix
bought thousands of acres in its wilderness,
where Dixfield in the west, and Dixmont in the

east, townships once owned by him, preserve his name and memory.

The house of Dr. Dix in Boston, called the "Dix Mansion," was on Washington St., corner of Dix Place, then Orange Court. It had a large garden behind it, where originated the Dix pear, once a favorite. Dr. Dix died in 1809, when Dorothea was seven years old. Young as she was, he was among the most vivid of her childhood memories and by far the pleasantest. She seems to have been a favorite with him and it was his delight to take her in his chaise on his rounds, talking playfully with her and listening to her childish prattle.

Joseph Dix, the father of Dorothea, is a vague and shadowy memory. He seems to have had little of his father's energy or good sense. Unstable in many of his ways, he lived a migratory life, "at various spots in Maine, New Hampshire, and Vermont, as well as in Worcester and Boston, Mass." When Dorothea was born, he was living at Hampden, Maine, adjoining his father's Dixmont properties, presumably as his father's land agent. He probably tired of this occupation because it interfered with his business. His business seems to have been religion. He was a prolific author of religious literature. He was a philanthropist after his kind, giving his time without stint to the writing of religious tracts, and spending his money in publishing them, with little benefit to the world and much detriment to his family. In the stitching and pasting of these tracts, the whole household were required to assist and it was against this irksome task-work that Dorothea, at the age of twelve, rebelled, running away from Worcester, where the family then lived, and finding a refuge with her grandmother in Boston. Dorothea afterwards educated her two brothers, one of whom became a sea captain and the other a Boston merchant.

Dorothea Dix was created by her Maker, but she was given in a plastic state, first into the hands of inexorable Madam Dix, and next into those of the all-pitying Dr. Channing. Madam Dix is described as a fine specimen of the dignified, precise, conscientious New England gentlewoman of her generation. Industry, economy, and above all thoroughness were the chief articles of her religion, and she instilled these virtues into the mind of her granddaughter by the most vigorous discipline. A week of solitary confinement was among the penalties inflicted upon the hapless child who had failed to reach the standard of duty prescribed for her. The standard, with Madam Dix, did not differ from perfection discernibly. Mr. Tiffany quotes a lady who in her girlhood, as a special reward of merit, was allowed to make an entire shirt under the supervision of Madam Dix. It was an experience never forgotten. No stitch in the entire garment could be allowed to differ perceptibly from every other, but the lady spoke of the ordeal with enthusiastic gratitude, declaring that it had been a life-long benefit to her to have been compelled to do one piece of work thoroughly well.

"I never knew childhood," Miss Dix said pitifully in after life. Certainly with this exacting grandmother, there can be no childhood as it is understood to-day; but if Dorothea submits to the rigorous discipline enforced upon her, she will make a woman of iron fibre who will flinch from no hardship and will leave no task undone. Happily she did submit to it. The alternative would have been to return to her half-vagabond father. Too much discipline or too little was her destiny. She preferred to take the medicine in excess, and in the end was grateful for it.

Dorothea was so apt a pupil and so ambitious that, at the age of fourteen, she returned to Worcester and opened a school for small children, prudently lengthening the skirts and sleeves of her dress to give dignity and impressiveness to her appearance. Half a century later one of these pupils vividly recalled the child-teacher, tall of her age, easily blushing, at once beautiful and imposing in manner, but inexorably strict in discipline.

Dorothea spent the next four years in Boston in preparation for a more ambitious undertaking and, in 1821 at the age of nineteen, she opened a day school in Boston in a small house belonging to Madam Dix. The school prospered and gradually expanded into a day and boarding school, for which the Dix mansion, whither the school was removed, furnished convenient space. Madam Dix, enfeebled by age and infirmities, laid down the scepter she had wielded, and the premises passed virtually into the hands of Dorothea. Thither came pupils from " the most prominent families in Boston " and other Massachusetts towns, and even from beyond the limits of the State. There also she brought her brothers to be educated under her care and started upon a business career.

Hardly had she started her school for the rich and fortunate before, anticipating her vocation as a philanthropist, she opened another for the poor and destitute. A letter is preserved in which she pleadingly asks the conscientious but perhaps stony Madam Dix for the loft over the stable for this purpose. " My dear grandmother," she begins, " Had I the saint-like eloquence of our minister, I would employ it in explaining all the motives, and dwelling on the good, the good to the poor, the miserable, the idle, the ignorant, which would follow your giving me permission to use the barn chamber for a school-room for charitable and religious purposes."

The minister with saint-like eloquence was Dr. Channing. The letter is valuable as showing the source of the flame that had fired her philanthropic soul. For the finer culture of the heart she had passed from the hands of Madam Dix to those of Dr. Channing. The request for the room was granted and Mr. Tiffany tells us that " The little barn-school proved the nucleus out of which years later was developed the beneficent work of the Warren Street Chapel, from which as a centre spread far and wide a new ideal of dealing with childhood. There first was interest excited in the mind of Rev. Charles Barnard, a man of positive spiritual genius in charming and uplifting the children of the poor and debased."

Letters from Miss Dix at this period show that she had a sensitive nature, easily wrought upon, now inflamed to action and now melted to tears. "You say that I weep easily. I was early taught to sorrow, to shed tears, and now, when sudden joy lights up or unexpected sorrow strikes my heart, I find it difficult to repress the full and swelling tide of feeling." She is reading a book of poems and weeping over it,—"paying my watery tribute to the genius" of the poet. She longs for similar talents that she " might revel in the luxury of those mental visions that must hourly entrance a spirit that partakes less of earth than heaven." It will be remembered that her father was religious even to folly. Here was his child, only by judicious training, the stream was turned into channels of wise beneficence.

With the management of two schools, the supervision of the household, the care of two younger brothers, and ministries to her grandmother already advanced in years, Miss Dix was sufficiently occupied, but she found time to prepare a text-book upon "Common Things," gathering the material as she wrote. This, her first attempt at book-making, issued in 1824, was kept in print forty-five years, and went to its sixtieth edition in 1869. It was followed the next year by "Hymns for Children" selected and altered, and by a book of devotions entitled, "Evening Hours." Lengthening the day at both ends, "rising before the sun and going to bed after midnight," working while others slept, gave time for these extra tasks. Nature exacted her usual penalties. In the third year of this arduous labor, threatenings of lung troubles appeared which, however, she defied even when "in conducting her classes she had to stand with one hand on a desk for support, and the other pressed hard to her side as though to repress a hard pain." Meanwhile she wrote a bosom friend: "There is in our nature a disposition to indulgence, a secret desire to escape from labor, which unless hourly combated will overcome the best faculties of our minds and paralyse our most useful powers. . . . I have often entertained a dread lest I should fall a victim to my besieger, and that fear has saved me thus far."

Besides the terror of lapsing into self-indul-

gence, she was stimulated to activity by the
care of her brothers, for one of whom she seems
to have felt special anxiety: " Oh, Annie," she
writes, " if that child is good, I care not how
humble his pathway in life. It is for him my
soul is filled with bitterness when sickness wastes
me; it is because of him I dread to die." Was
there no one to advise her that the best care
of her brother would be to care for herself, and
that if she would do more, she must first do less!
Where was Dr. Channing who, more than any
other, was responsible for her intemperate zeal!
It appears that Dr. Channing, " not without
solicitude," as he writes her, was watching over
his eager disciple. " Your infirm health," he
says, " seems to darken your prospect of usefulness. But I believe your constitution will
yet be built up, if you will give it a fair chance.
You must learn to give up your plans of usefulness as much as those of gratification, to the
will of God."

Miss Dix abandoned her school apparently
in 1827, after six years of service and at the
age of twenty-five. The following spring and
summer she spent as a governess in the family
of Dr. Channing at his summer home in Rhode
Island. Her duties were light and she lived

much in the open air, devoting her leisure to botany in which she was already " no mean proficient," and to " the marine life of the beautiful region." Very pretty letters were exchanged between her and Dr. Channing at the termination of the engagement. "We will hear no more of thanks," he wrote her, " but your affection for us and our little ones we will treasure among our most precious blessings." He invites her to renew the relations another year, and so she did.

To avoid the rigors of a New England climate, Miss Dix, for some years, spent her winters, now in Philadelphia, now in Alexandria, Va., keeping herself busy with reading " of a very multifarious kind,— poetry, science, biography, and travels,— besides eking out the scanty means she had laid by from her teaching by writing stories and compiling floral albums and books of devotion." In 1827, she published a volume of " Ten Short Stories for Children " which went to a second edition in 1832; in 1828, " Meditations for Private Hours," which went through several editions; in 1829, two little books, " The Garland of Flora," and " The Pearl, a Christmas Gift."

Occasional brief engagements in teaching are also recorded in this period.

The winter of 1830, she spent with the Channings on the Island of St. Croix, in the West Indies, in her old capacity as governess. A daughter of Dr. Channing gives an interesting account of the preceptress of whom, first and last, she had seen so much. She describes Miss Dix as tall and dignified, very shy in manner, strict and inflexible in discipline. " From her iron will, it was hopeless to appeal. I think she was a very accomplished teacher, active and diligent herself, very fond of natural history and botany. She enjoyed long rambles, always calling our attention to what was interesting in the world around us. I hear that some of her pupils speak of her as irascible. I have no such remembrance. Fixed as fate we considered her."

Miss Dix returned from the West Indies in the spring, very much improved in health, and in the autumn, she reopened her school in the Dix Mansion, with the same high ideals as before and with such improved methods as experience had suggested. Pupils came to her again as of old and she soon had as many attendants as her space permitted. A feature of the school was a letter-box through which passed a daily mail between teacher and pupils and "large bundles of child-letters of this period" are still extant, preserved by Miss Dix with scrupulous care to the end of life. It was a bright child who wrote as follows: "I thought I was doing well until I read your letter, but when you said that you were rousing to greater energy, all my satisfaction vanished. For if you are not satisfied in some measure with yourself and are going to do more than you have done, I don't know what I shall do. You do not go to rest until midnight and then you rise very early." The physician had administered too strong a tonic for the little patient's health.

A lady who, at the age of sixteen, attended this school in 1833, writes of her eminent teacher as follows: "She fascinated me from the first, as she had done many of my class before me. Next to my mother, I thought her the most beautiful woman I had ever seen. She was in the prime of her years, tall and of dignified carriage, head finely shaped and set, with an abundance of soft, wavy, brown hair. The school continued in the full tide of success for five years, during which time, by hard labor and close economies, Miss Dix had saved enough to secure her " the independence of a modest competence." This seems a great achievement, but if one spends nothing for superfluities and does most of his labor himself, he can lay by his income, much or little. The appointments of the school are said to have been very simple, a long table serving as a desk for study, when it was not in use for dinner. Only one assistant is mentioned, who gave instruction in French and, perhaps, elementary Latin. Surely Miss Dix could handle the rest herself. The merit of the school was not in its elaborate appointments, but in the personal supervision of its accomplished mistress. So the miracle was wrought and at the age of thirty-three, Miss Dix had achieved a modest competence.

The undertaking had cost her her health once before, and now it cost her her health again. The old symptoms, a troublesome cough, pain in the side, and slight hemorrhages, returned and, having dragged her frail body through the winter of 1836, Miss Dix reluctantly closed her school in the spring and, in obedience to her physician, went to Europe for rest, with the intention of spending the summer in England, the autumn in France, and the winter in Italy. Prostrated by the voyage, she was carried to a hotel in Liverpool where she was put to bed with the forlorn prospect of being confined to her solitary room for an indefinite period of convalescence. But again Dr. Channing befriended her. From him she had received letters of introduction, one of which brought to her side Mr. William Rathbone, a wealthy merchant of Liverpool and a prominent English Unitarian. Mr. and Mrs. Rathbone insisted upon taking her to their home, a charming residence a few miles out of the city. Thither she consented to go for a visit of a few weeks, and there she remained, as an honored guest tenderly cared for, for eighteen months. " To the end of her days," says her biographer, " this period of eighteen months stood out in her memory as the jubilee of her life, the sunniest, the most restful, and the tenderest to her affections of her whole earthly experience." She wrote a Boston friend, " You must imagine me surrounded by every comfort, sustained by every tenderness that can cheer, blest in the continual kindness of the family in which Providence has placed me,— I with no claim but those of a common nature." And again, " So completely am I adopted into the circle of loving spirits that I sometimes forget

I really am not to consider the bonds transient in their binding."

She very much needed these friends and their tender care. Nine months after her arrival, we hear of occasional hemorrhages from which she has been exempt for ten days, the pain in her side less acute, and her physician has given her permission to walk about her room. One would think that her career was practically ended, but, strange to say, the career which was to make her famous had not yet begun. From this date, her convalescence proceeded steadily, and she was able to enjoy much in the delightful home and refined social circle in which she found herself. " Your remark," she writes a friend, " that I probably enjoy more now in social intercourse than I have ever before done is quite true. Certainly if I do not improve, it will be through wilful self-neglect." Apparently, she was having a glimpse of a less prosaic existence than the grinding routine of a boarding school. Madam Dix died at the age of ninety-one, leaving her granddaughter, still in Europe, a substantial legacy, which sensibly increased her limited resources and, when the time came for action, left her free to carry out her great schemes of benevolence without hampering personal anx-

icties. It ought to preserve the memory of
Madam Dix that she endowed a great philanthropist.

In the autumn of 1837, Miss Dix returned to
America, and avoiding the New England climate, spent the winter in Washington, D. C.,
and its neighborhood. Apparently, it was not
a wholly happy winter, chiefly because of her
vain and tender longings for the paradise she
had left across the sea. The Washington of
1837 seemed raw to her after the cultivated
English home she had discovered. " I was not
conscious," she writes a friend, " that so great
a trial was to meet my return from England till
the whole force of the contrast was laid before
me. . . . I may be too craving of that rich
gift, the power of sharing with other minds.
I have drunk deeply, long, and Oh, how bliss-
fully, at this fountain in a foreign clime.
Hearts met hearts, minds joined with minds, and
what were the secondary trials of pain to the
enfeebled body when daily was administered the
soul's medicine and food." Surely, that English experience was one upon which not every
invalid from these shores could count, but when,
a few years later, Miss Dix returned to England
as a kind of angel of mercy, giving back much

more than she had ever received, the Rathbone family must have been glad that they had befriended her in her obscurity and her need.

It was in 1841 at the age of thirty-nine that the second chapter in the life of Miss Dix began. Note that she had as little thought that she was beginning a great career as any one of us that he will date all his future from something he has done or experienced to-day. It happened that Dr. J. T. G. Nichols, so long the beloved pastor of the Unitarian parish in Saco, Maine, was then a student of Divinity at Cambridge. He had engaged to assist in a Sunday School in the East Cambridge jail, and all the women, twenty in number, had been assigned to him. The experience of one session with his class was enough to convince him that a young man was very much out of place in that position and that a woman, sensible if possible, but a woman certainly, was necessary. His mother advised him to consult Miss Dix. Not that her health would permit her to take the class, but she could advise. On hearing Mr. Nichols' statement, Miss Dix deliberated a moment and then said, " I will take the class myself." Mr. Nichols protested that this was not to be thought of, in the condition of her health, but we have heard of her iron will: " Fixed as fate we considered her," said one of her pupils; and she answered Mr. Nichols, " I shall be there next Sunday."

This was the beginning. " After the school was over," says Dr. Nichols, " Miss Dix went into the jail and found among the prisoners a few insane persons with whom she talked. She noticed that there was no stove in their rooms and no means of proper warmth." The date was the twenty-eighth of March and the climate was New England, from which Miss Dix had so often had to flee. " The jailer said that a fire for them was not needed, and would be unsafe. Her repeated solicitations were without success." The jailer must have thought he was dealing with a woman, not with destiny. " At that time the court was in session at East Cambridge, and she caused the case to be brought before it. Her request was granted. The cold rooms were warmed. Thus was her great work commenced."

Such is Dr. Nichols' brief statement, but the course of events did not run so smoothly as we are led to suppose. The case had to be fought through the newspapers as well as the court, and here Miss Dix showed the generalship which she exhibited on many another hard fought field. She never went into battle single-handed. She always managed to have at her side the best gunners when the real battle began. In the East Cambridge skirmish, she had Rev. Robert C. Waterston, Dr. Samuel G. Howe, and Charles Sumner. Dr. Howe visited the jail and wrote an account for the Boston *Advertiser*. When this statement was disputed, as it was, Mr. Sumner, who had accompanied Dr. Howe, confirmed his account and added details of his own. He said that the inmates " were cramped together in rooms poorly ventilated and noisome with filth;" that " in two cages or pens constructed of plank, within the four stone walls of the same room " were confined, and had been for months, a raving maniac and an interesting young woman whose mind was so slightly obscured that it seemed any moment as if the cloud would pass away; that " the whole prison echoed with the blasphemies of the poor old woman, while her young and gentle fellow in suffering seemed to shrink from her words as from blows;" that the situation was hardly less horrid than that of " tying the living to the dead."

Where was Miss Dix during this controversy? Why, she was preparing to investigate every jail and almshouse in the State of Massachusetts. If this was the way the insane were treated in the city of Cambridge, in a community distinguished for enlightenment and humanity, what might not be going on in more backward and less favored localities? Note-book in hand, going from city to city and from town to town, Miss Dix devoted the two following years to answering this question exhaustively.

Having gathered her facts, she presented them to the Legislature in a Memorial of thirty-two octavo pages, the first of a series of seventeen statements and appeals presented to the legislatures of different states, as far west as Illinois and as far south as Louisiana. " I shall be obliged," she said, " to speak with great plainness and to reveal many things revolting to the taste, and from which my woman's nature shrinks with peculiar sensitiveness. . . . I proceed, gentlemen, briefly to call your attention to the present state of insane persons within this Commonwealth, in cages, closets, cellars, stalls, pens, chained, naked, beaten with rods and lashed into obedience. . . . I give a few illustrations but description fades before reality." If we could dismiss the subject by saying she reports instance after instance where men and women were confined in the almshouses in Massachusetts in such conditions of inhumanity and neglect as no intelligent farmer would tolerate for his swine, we could avoid some unpleasant details; but the statement would be ineffective because it would seem incredible. At the almshouse in Danvers, confined in a remote, low, outbuilding, she found a young woman, once respectable, industrious and worthy, whose mind had been deranged by disappointments and trials. " There she stood," says Miss Dix, " clinging to or beating upon the bars of her caged apartment, the contracted size of which afforded space only for increasing accumulations of filth,—a foul spectacle; there she stood, with naked arms, dishevelled hair, the unwashed frame invested with fragments of unclean garments, the air so extremely offensive, though ventilation was afforded on all sides but one, that it was not possible to remain beyond a few moments without retreating for recovery to the outward air. Irritation of body, produced by utter filth and exposure, incited her to the horrid process of tearing off her skin by inches; her neck and person were thus disfigured to hideousness. . . . And who protects her," Miss Dix suggestively asks, " who protects her,— that worse than Pariah outcast,—from other wrongs and blacker outrages!" This question had more meaning for Miss Dix than we might suppose, for at the almshouse in Worcester she had found an insane Madonna and her babe: father unknown.

Fair and beautiful Newton finds a place in this chapter of dishonor, with a woman chained, nearly nude, and filthy beyond measure: " Sick, horror-struck, and almost incapable of retreating, I gained the outward air." A case in Groton attained infamous celebrity, not because the shame was without parallel but because the overseers of the poor tried to discredit the statements of Miss Dix. The fact was that she had understated the case. Dr. Bell of the McLean Asylum, confirmed her report and added details. In an outbuilding at the almshouse, a young man, slightly deranged but entirely inoffensive, was confined by a heavy iron collar to which was attached a chain six feet in length, the limit of his possible movements. His hands were fastened together by heavy clavises secured by iron bolts. There was no window in his dungeon, but for ventilation there was an opening, half the size of a sash, closed in cold weather by a board shutter. From this cell, he had been

[146]

taken to the McLean Asylum, where his irons had been knocked off, his swollen limbs chafed gently, and finding himself comfortable, he exclaimed, " My good man, I must kiss you." He showed no violence, ate at the common table, slept in the common bed-room, and seemed in a fair way to recovery when, to save the expense of three dollars a week for his board and care, the thrifty Groton officials took him away. He could be boarded at the alms-house for nothing, and, chained in an outbuilding, he would not require any care.

We can follow Miss Dix in her career through a dozen states of this Union, into the British Provinces, to Scotland and England, thence across to the Continent, without repeating these details, if we bear in mind that such as we have seen was the condition of the pauper insane at that period. Her memorial was presented by Dr. S. G. Howe, then happily a member of the Legislature, and a bill was passed, not without opposition, but finally passed, enlarging the asylum at Worcester to accommodate two hundred additional patients. The provision was inadequate, but a reform of old abuses had begun. It was her first victory.

Grateful for what had been accomplished in

Massachusetts, Miss Dix turned to Rhode Island, whose borders she had often approached and sometimes crossed in her investigations in the adjoining state. Rhode Island was perhaps not less civilized than her neighbor, but Rhode Island furnished the prize case of horrors in the mistreatment of insanity, a case which in a letter introducing the discoverer, Mr. Thomas G. Hazard said went beyond anything he supposed to exist in the civilized world. The case was this: Abraham Simmons, a man whose name ought to go on the roll of martyrdom, was confined in the town of Little Compton, in a cell seven feet square, stone-built, stone-roofed, and stone-floored, the entrance double-walled, double-doored and double-locked, " excluding both light and fresh air, and without accommodation of any description for warming and ventilation." When this dungeon was discovered, the walls were covered by frost a half inch in thickness; the bed was provided with two comfortables, both wet and the outer one stiffly frozen, or, as Miss Dix puts it, " only wet straw to lie upon and a sheet of ice for his covering." Lest two locks should not be enough to hold this dangerous man, his leg was tethered to the stone floor by an ox-chain. " My husband," said the mistress, " in winter, sometimes of a morning rakes out half a bushel of frost, *and yet he never freezes;* sometimes he screams dreadfully and that is the reason we had the double wall and two doors in place of one; his cries disturb us in the house." " How long has he been here? " " Oh, above three years." Nothing in the traditions of the Bastile could exceed these horrors, and yet they were not the product of intentional cruelty, but of unfathomable stupidity.

Disregarding the well-meant warnings of her attendant that he would kill her, Miss Dix took his hands, tried to warm them in her own, spoke to him of liberty, care and kindness, and for answer " a tear stole over his hollow cheeks, but no words answered my importunities." Her next step was to publish the terrible story in the Providence Journal, not with a shriek, as might have been expected and justified, but with the affected coolness of a naturalist. With grim humor, she headed her article, " Astonishing Tenacity of Life," as if it had only a scientific interest for anybody. If you doubted the statements, you might go and see for yourself: " Should any persons in this philanthropic age be disposed from motives of curiosity to visit the place, they may rest assured that travelling is

[149]

considered quite safe in that part of the country, however improbable it may seem. The people of that region profess the Christian religion, and it is even said that they have adopted some forms and ceremonies which they call worship. It is not probable, however, that they address themselves to poor Simmons' God." Their prayers and his shrieks would make a strange discord, she thinks, if they entered the ear of the same deity.

Having reported her discoveries to the men of science, she next appealed to the men of wealth. Providence had at that date a multi-millionaire, by the name of Butler; he left four millions to his heirs. He had never been known as a philanthropist; he did not himself suppose that his heart was susceptible. It is said that knowing persons smiled when they heard that Miss Dix intended to appeal to him. Further, it is said that Mr. Butler, at the interview, ingeniously diverted the conversation from topics that threatened to be serious. He apparently had no thought of giving Miss Dix a penny. At length she rose with the impressive dignity so often noted by her pupils and said: " Mr. Butler, I wish you to hear what I have to say. I want to bring before you certain facts involving terrible suffering to your fellow creatures all around you,— suffering you can relieve. My duty will end when I have done this, and with you will rest all further responsibility." Mr. Butler heard her respectfully to the end, and then asked, "What do you want me to do?" "Sir," she said, "I want you to give $50,000 toward the enlargement of the insane hospital in this city." "Madam, I'll do it," he said, and much more of his estate afterward went the same way.

Three years of devoted study of the problems of insanity, with limitless opportunities for personal observation, had given Miss Dix an expert knowledge of the subject. She had conceived what an insane asylum should be. Hitherto, she had been content to enlarge upon foundations already laid; now she would build an asylum herself. She saw, we are told, that such an institution as she conceived could not be built by private benevolence, but must have behind it a legislative appropriation. She chose New Jersey as the field of her experiment. Quietly, she entered the state and canvassed its jails and almshouses, as she had those of Massachusetts and Rhode Island. Next she digested her facts in a Memorial to the Legislature. Then, with

a political shrewdness for which she became celebrated, she selected the member, uniting a good
heart with a clear head and persistent will, into
whose hands it should be placed. Much of her
success is said to have been due to her political
sagacity. The superintendent of one of her asylums said, "She had an insight into character
that was truly marvellous; and I have never
known anyone, man or woman, who bore more
distinctly the mark of intellectuality." Having
placed her Memorial in the hands of a skilful
tactician, she retired to a room appropriated to
her use by the courtesy of the House, where she
spent her time writing editorials for newspapers,
answering the questions of members, and holding receptions. "You cannot imagine," she
writes a friend, "the labor of conversing and
convincing. Some evenings I had at once twenty gentlemen for three hours' steady conversation." After a campaign of two months the
bill establishing the New Jersey State Lunatic
Asylum was passed, and the necessary money
appropriated for its erection. She was always
partial to this first creation of her energy and
genius. She called it 'her first child,' and
there, forty-five years later, she returned to pass
the last seven years of her life, as in a home, a

room having been gratefully appropriated to her use by the trustees of the asylum.

At this date, Dr. S. G. Howe wrote her: "God grant me to look back upon some three years of my life with a part of the self-approval you must feel. I ask no higher fortune. No one need say to you, Go on! for you have heard a higher than any human voice, and you will follow whithersoever it calleth." Indeed, she already had much of her future work prepared. While waiting for the Legislature in New Jersey to take up her bill, she had canvassed Pennsylvania and had the happiness to see a bill pass the Legislature of that State founding the Dixmont Hospital, her second child, soon after the birth of her first. The Dixmont Hospital is the only one of her many children that she would allow to be even indirectly named for her. Meanwhile, she had canvassed Kentucky, had been before the Legislature in Tennessee, and, seven days after the passage of her bill in New Jersey, she writes from a steamer near Charleston, S. C., as follows: "I designed using the spring and summer chiefly in examining the jails and poorhouses of Indiana and Illinois. Having successfully completed my mission in Kentucky, I learned that traveling in those

States would be difficult, if not impossible, for some weeks to come, on account of mud and rains. This decided me to examine the prisons and hospitals of New Orleans, and, returning, to see the state prisons of Louisiana at Baton Rouge, of Mississippi at Jackson, of Arkansas at Little Rock, of Missouri at Jefferson City, and of Illinois at Alton. . . . I have seen incomparably more to approve than to censure in New Orleans. I took the resolution, being so far away, of seeing the state institutions of Georgia, Alabama, and South Carolina. Though this has proved excessively fatiguing, I rejoice that I have carried out my purpose."

Between June 1843 and August 1847, she states in a letter that she traveled 32,470 miles, her conveyance being by steamboat when possible; otherwise by stage-coach. It is suggestive of the wrecks and delays she had experienced with the shattered coaches and mud roads of the south and west that, as we are told, she " made a practice of carrying with her an outfit of hammer, wrench, nails, screws, a coil of rope, and straps of stout leather, which under many a mishap sufficed to put things to rights and enable her to pursue her journey." " I have encountered nothing so dangerous as river fords," she writes. " I crossed the Yadkin when it was three-quarters of a mile wide, rough bottom, often in places rapid currents; the water always up to the carriage bed, and sometimes flowing in. The horses rested twice on sand-bars. A few miles beyond the river having just crossed a deep branch two hundred yards wide, the axletree broke, and away rolled one of the back wheels."

When she said that river fords were her greatest danger, she must have forgotten an encounter with a highwayman. She was making a stage journey in Michigan, and noticed with some consternation that the driver carried a brace of pistols. To her inquiries he explained that there had been robberies on the road. " Give me the pistols," she said; " I will take care of them." More in awe of her than of robbers, the driver reluctantly obeyed. Passing through a dismal forest the expected happened. A man seized the horses and demanded her purse. She made him a little speech, asked if he was not ashamed, told him her business, and concluded, " If you have been unfortunate, are in distress and in want of money, I will give you some." Meanwhile the robber had turned " deathly pale," and when she had finished, exclaimed, " My God, that voice." He had once heard her address the prisoners in the Philadelphia penitentiary. He begged her to pass, and declined to take the money she offered. She insisted, lest he might be again tempted before he found employment. People obeyed when she insisted, and he took her gift and disappeared.

Think of the hotel accommodations,— the tables and beds,— she must have encountered in these wild journeys. This is the woman who, a few years ago, seemed to be dying with hemorrhages of the lungs. Did she have no more of them? Oh, yes; we are assured that " again and again she was attacked with hemorrhages and again and again prostrated by malarial fever." A physician said, " Her system became actually saturated with malaria." Invalid as she almost always was, she had left her foot-prints in most of the states of the Union and had carried the war into the British Provinces, where she had been the means of establishing three insane hospitals: one in Toronto, one in Halifax, one at St. John, Newfoundland, besides providing a fleet of life-boats at Sable Island, known as " The Graveyard of Ships," off the coast of Nova Scotia.

In the United States, during these twelve

years, she " promoted and secured," to use her own phrase, the enlargement of three asylums: at Worcester, Mass., at Providence, R.I., and at Utica, N. Y., and the establishment of thirteen, one in each of the following states: New Jersey, Pennsylvania, Indiana, Illinois, Kentucky, Missouri, Tennessee, Mississippi, Louisiana, Alabama, North Carolina, and Maryland, with the Hospital for Insane Soldiers and Sailors, at Washington, D. C.

In 1850, Miss Dix proposed a larger scheme of philanthropy than was ever before projected by any mortal. What is more, but for one man, she would have carried it out. She petitioned Congress to appropriate 12,000,000 acres of public lands for the benefit of the indigent insane, deaf and dumb, and blind. A bill to that effect was introduced, watched by her through two sessions, and finally passed by both Houses. She was inundated with congratulations from far and near; but the bill was vetoed on constitutional grounds by President Pierce. The day for giving away the public lands in sheets had not come.

The blow seems to have been more than Miss Dix could endure. She went abroad for change

and rest.   What rest meant to her, she expresses
in a letter to a friend at home:

> " Rest is not quitting the active career:
>   Rest is the fitting of self to its sphere."

These lines, borrowed from John S. Dwight
have been, not unnaturally, attributed to her.
She wrote many things perhaps quite as poetical.

Not much of the verse, which came from her
prolific pen, was considered even by herself to
deserve publication, but verse-writing is said to
had been the never-failing diversion of her
leisure hours. Mrs. Caroline A. Kennard
credits her with the following lines which,
though very simple, are quite as good as much
that has been immortalized in our hymn books:

> " In the tender, peaceful moonlight,
>   I am from the world apart,
> While a flood of golden glory
>   Fills alike my room and heart.
>
> As I gaze upon the radiance
>   Shining on me from afar,
> I can almost see beyond it,—
>   Almost see ' the gates ajar.'

Tender thoughts arise within me
  Of the friends who've gone before,
Absent long but not forgotten,
  Resting on the other shore.

And my soul is filled with longing
  That when done with earth and sin,
I may find the gates wide open
  There for me to enter in."

Apparently, she wrote her poetry for herself, as an unskilled musician might play for his own amusement.

The rest which Miss Dix allowed herself between September 1854 and September 1856, was to visit the chief hospitals and prisons in Europe. Edinburg, the Channel Islands, Paris, Rome, Naples, Constantinople, Vienna, St. Petersburg, Stockholm, Copenhagen, Amsterdam, Brussels, and again Paris and London: these places mark the course of her two years' pilgrimage among the prisons and hospitals of Europe. She found much to admire in this journey, but sometimes abuses to correct. We must content ourselves with an incident from Edinburg, perfectly in character. She found in that city private insane hospitals, if they could be dignified by the name, under such conditions of mismanagement as shocked even her experienced nerves. Having reported the facts to the Lord Provost of Edinburg to no purpose, she was advised to lay the matter before the Home Secretary in London. The Provost knew of this intention and resolved to forestall her by taking the train for London the next morning; so little did he know Miss Dix. She boarded the night train, and was on the spot before him, had her interview, secured the appointment of a royal commission and, ultimately the correction of the abuses of which she had complained.

During the four years that intervened between her return and the outbreak of the Civil War, she seems to have travelled over most of her old ground in this country, and to have extended her journeys into the new states and territories. At the approach of hostilities, it fell to Miss Dix to give the President of the Philadelphia and Baltimore Railroad the first information of a plot to capture the city of Washington and to assassinate Mr. Lincoln. Acting upon this information, Gen. Butler's Massachusetts troops were sent by boat instead of rail, and Mr. Lincoln was " secretly smuggled through to Washington."

By natural selection, Miss Dix was appointed Superintendent of Women Nurses in the federal service, by order of the Secretary of War. In this capacity she served through the four years' struggle. In a letter dated December 7, 1864, she writes: "I take no hour's leisure. I think that since the war, I have taken no day's furlough." Her great services were officially recognized by Edwin M. Stanton, Secretary of War.

Having served the country as faithfully as any soldier, during its hour of need, she returned to her former work of promoting and securing the erection of hospitals and of visiting those before established. In 1877, when Miss Dix was seventy-five, Dr. Charles F. Folsom, of Boston, in a book entitled " Diseases of the Mind," said of her: " Her frequent visits to our institutions of the insane now, and her searching criticisms, constitute of themselves a better lunacy commission than would be likely to be appointed in many of our states."

She was at that date, however, near the end of her active labors. In 1881, at the age of seventy-nine, she retired to the hospital she had been the means of building in Trenton, N. J., and there she remained, tenderly, even reverently cared for, until her death in 1887. So passed to her rest and her reward one of the most remarkable women of her generation.

V
SARAH MARGARET FULLER
OSSOLI

SARAH MARGARET FULLER OSSOLI

At Cambridge, it is still possible to pick up interesting reminiscences of Longfellow and Lowell from old neighbors or townsmen, proud even to have seen these celebrities as familiar objects upon the street. "And Margaret Fuller," you suggest, further to tap the memory of your venerable friend. He smiles gently and says, Margaret Fuller was before his time; he remembers the table-talk of his youth. He remembers, when she was a girl at dancing-school, Papanti stopped his class and said, "Mees Fuller, Mees Fuller, you sal not be so magnee-fee-cent"; he remembers that, being asked if she thought herself better than any one else, she calmly said, "Yes, I do"; and he remembers that Miss Fuller having announced that she accepted the universe, a wit remarked that the universe ought to be greatly obliged to her.

Margaret Fuller was born in 1810, a year later than Longfellow, but while Longfellow lived until 1882, Margaret was lost at sea thirty years before, in 1850. The last four years of her life were spent in Italy, so that American memories of Margaret must needs go back to 1846. Practically it is traditions of her that remain, and not memories. As she survives in tradition, she seems to have been a person of inordinate vanity, who gave lectures in drawing-rooms and called them " conversations," uttered a commonplace with the authority of an oracle, and sentimentalized over art, poetry, or religion, while she seemed to herself, and apparently to others, to be talking philosophy. She took herself in all seriousness as a genius, ran a dazzling career of a dozen years or so in Cambridge and Boston, and then her light seems to have gone out. She came to the surface, with other newness, in the Transcendental era; she was the priestess of its mysteries; when that movement ebbed away, her day was over. This is the impression one would gather, if he had only current oral traditions of Margaret Fuller.

If with this impression, wishing to get a first-hand knowledge of his subject, a student were to read the " Works of Margaret Fuller " : — " Life Within and Without," " At Home and Abroad," " Woman in the Nineteenth Century," " Art, Literature, and Drama,"— he would be prepared to find eccentricities of style, straining

SARAH MARGARET FULLER OSSOLI

for effect, mystical utterances, attempts at profundity, and stilted commonplace. He would, however, find nothing of this sort, or of any sort of make believe, but simply a writer always in earnest, always convinced, with a fair English style, perfectly intelligible, intent upon conveying an idea in the simplest manner and generally an idea which approves itself to the common-sense of the reader. There is no brilliancy, no ornament, little imagination, and not a least glimmer of wit. The absence of wit is remarkable, since in conversation, wit was a quality for which Margaret was both admired and feared. But as a writer, Margaret was a little prosaic,— even her poetry inclined to be prosaic,— but she is earnest, noble, temperate, and reasonable. The reader will be convinced that there was more in the woman than popular tradition recognizes.

One is confirmed in the conviction that the legend does her less than justice when he knows the names and the quality of her friends. No woman ever had better or more loyal friends than Margaret Fuller. Ralph Waldo Emerson, James Freeman Clarke and William Henry Channing were among them and compiled her " Memoirs," evidently as a labor of love.

George William Curtis knew her personally, and called her " a scholar, a critic, a thinker, a queen of conversation, above all, a person of delicate insight and sympathy, of the most feminine refinement of feeling and of dauntless courage." Col. Higginson, a fellow-townsman, who from youth to manhood, knew Margaret personally, whose sisters were her intimates, whose family, as he tells us, was " afterwards closely connected " with hers by marriage, and who has studied all the documents and written her biography, says she was a " person whose career is more interesting, as it seems to me, than that of any other American of her sex; a woman whose aims were high and whose services great; one whose intellect was uncommon, whose activity was incessant, whose life, varied, and whose death, dramatic."

There still remains the current legend, and a legend, presumably, has some foundation. If we attempt to unite the Margaret Fuller of common tradition with Margaret Fuller as estimated by her friends, we shall assume that she was not a wholly balanced character,— that she must have been a great and noble woman to have had such friends, but that there may have been in her some element of foolishness which her friends excused and at which the public smiled.

Margaret was the fifth in descent from Lieut. Thomas Fuller, who came from England in 1638, and who celebrated the event in a poem of which the first stanza is as follows:

> " In thirty-eight I set my foot
>   On this New England shore;
> My thoughts were then to stay one year,
>   And then remain no more."

The poetry is on a level with other colonial poetry of the period.

Timothy Fuller, the grandfather of Margaret, graduated at Harvard College in 1760, became a clergyman, and was a delegate to the Massachusetts State Convention which adopted the Federal Constitution. He had five sons, all of whom became lawyers. " They were in general," says Col. Higginson, " men of great energy, pushing, successful, of immense and varied information, of great self-esteem, and without a particle of tact." The evidence is that Margaret reproduced, in a somewhat exaggerated form, all these Fuller characteristics, good and bad. The saying is quoted from Horace Mann that if Margaret was unpopular,

" it was because she probably inherited the disagreeableness of forty Fullers."

Timothy Fuller, Margaret's father, was the oldest of these brothers and, Col. Higginson says, " the most successful and the most assured." He graduated at Harvard, second in his class, in 1801, lived in Cambridge, and represented the Middlesex district in Congress from 1817 to 1825. He was a " Jeffersonian Democrat " and a personal friend and political supporter of John Quincy Adams. He married Margaret, the daughter of Major Peter Crane. Mrs. Fuller was as gentle and unobtrusive as her stalwart husband was forceful and uncompliant. She effaced herself even in her own home, was seen and not heard, though apparently not very conspicuously seen. She had eight children, of whom Margaret was the first, and when this busy mother escaped from the care of the household, it was to take refuge in her flower garden. A " fair blossom of the white amaranth," Margaret calls this mother. The child's nature took something from both of her parents, and was both strong and tender.

Her father assumed the entire charge of Margaret's education, setting her studying Latin at the age of six, not an unusual feat in that day for a boy, but hitherto unheard of for a girl. Her lessons were recited at night, after Mr. Fuller returned from his office in Boston, often at a late hour. "High-pressure," says Col. Higginson, "is bad enough for an imaginative and excitable child, but high-pressure by candle-light is ruinous; yet that was the life she lived." The effect of these night lessons was to leave the child's brain both tired and excited and in no condition to sleep. It was considered singular that she was never ready for bed. She was hustled off to toss on her pillow, to see horrid visions, to have nightmare, and sometimes to walk in her sleep. Terrible morning headaches followed, and Margaret was considered a delicate child. One would like to know what Latin at six would have done for her, without those recitations by candle-light.

Mr. Fuller did not consider it important that a child should have juvenile books and Margaret's light reading consisted of Shakspere, Cervantes, and Molière. She gives an interesting account of her discovery of Shakspere at the age of eight. Foraging for entertainment on a dismal winter Sunday afternoon, she took down a volume of Shakspere and was soon lost in the adventures and misadventures of Romeo and Juliet. Two hours passed, when the child's exceeding quiet attracted attention. "That is no book for Sunday," said her father, "put it away." Margaret obeyed, but soon took the book again to follow the fortunes of her lovers further. This was a fatal indiscretion; the forbidden volume was again taken from her and she was sent to bed as a punishment for disobedience.

Meanwhile, the daily lessons to her father or to a private tutor went on; Virgil, Horace and Ovid were read in due course, and the study of Greek was begun. Margaret never forgave her father for robbing her of a proper childhood and substituting a premature scholastic education. "I certainly do not wish," she says, "that instead of these masters, I had read baby books, written down to children, but I do wish that I had read no books at all till later,— that I had lived with toys and played in the open air."

Her early and solitary development entailed disadvantages which only a very thoughtful parent could have foreseen. When, later, Margaret was sent to school, she had no companions in study, being in advance of the girls of her age, with whom she played, and too young for the older set with whom she was called to recite. " Not only," she says, " I was not their school-mate, but my book-life and lonely habits had given a cold aloofness to my whole expression, and veiled my manner with a hauteur which turned all hearts away."

The effects of her training upon her health, Margaret appears to have exaggerated. She thought it had " checked her growth, wasted her constitution," and would bring her to a " premature grave." While her lessons to her father by candle-light continued, there were sleeplessness, bad dreams, and morning head-aches, but after this had gone on one year, Mr. Fuller was elected to Congress, spent most of his time in Washington, and a private tutor gave the lessons, presumably at seasonable hours. No one with a " broken constitution " could have performed her later literary labors, and she was not threatened with a " premature grave " when Dr. Frederick Henry Hedge made her acquaintance in Cambridge society. "Mar-garet," he says, " was then about thirteen,— a child in years, but so precocious in her mental and physical development, that she passed for eighteen or twenty. Agreeably to this esti-mate, she had her place in society as a full-grown lady. When I recall her personal appearance as she was then, and for ten or twelve years subsequent, I have the idea of a blooming girl of florid complexion and vigorous health, with a tendency to robustness of which she was painfully conscious, and which, with little regard to hygienic principles, she endeavored to suppress and conceal, thereby preparing for herself much future suffering." She had, he says, " no pretensions to beauty then, or at any time," yet she " was not plain," a reproach from which she was saved " by her blond and abundant hair, by her excellent teeth, by her sparkling, dancing, busy eyes," and by a " graceful and peculiar carriage of her head and neck." He adds that " in conversation she had already, at that early age, begun to distinguish herself, and made much the same impression in society that she did in after years," but that she had an excessive " tendency to sarcasm " which frightened shy young people and made her notoriously unpopular with the ladies.

At this period Margaret attended a seminary for young ladies in Boston. Cambridge was then, according to Col. Higginson, a vast, sparsely settled village, containing between two and three thousand inhabitants. In the Boston school, Dr. Hedge says, " the inexperienced country girl was exposed to petty persecutions from the dashing misses of the city," and Margaret paid them off by " indiscriminate sarcasms."

Margaret's next two years were spent at a boarding school in Groton. Her adventures in this school are supposed to be narrated in her dramatic story entitled " Mariana," in the volume called " Summer on the Lakes." Mariana at first carried all before her " by her love of wild dances and sudden song, her freaks of passion and wit," but abusing her privileges, she is overthrown by her rebellious subjects, brought to great humiliation, and receives some needed moral instructions.

At fifteen, Margaret returned to Cambridge and resumed her private studies, except that, for a Greek recitation, she attended an academy in which Dr. Oliver Wendell Holmes was then fitting for college. Her day at this period, as she gives it, was occupied thus: she rose before five, walked an hour, and practiced at the piano till seven: breakfasted and read French till eight; read Brown's philosophy, two or three lectures, till half past nine; went to school and studied Greek till twelve; recited, went home,

and practiced till two; dined; lounged half an
hour, read two hours in Italian, walked or rode,
and spent her evenings leisurely with music or
friends.   Plainly she ought to have been one of
the learned women of her generation.

A school composition of Margaret impressed
her fellow pupil, Dr. Holmes, as he relates, with
a kind of awe.   It began loftily with the words,
" It is a trite remark," a phrase which seemed to
the boy very masterful.   The girls·envied her a
certain queenliness of manner.   " We thought,"
says one of them, " that if we could only come
into school in that way, we could know as much
Greek as she did."   She was accustomed to fill
the hood of her cloak with books, swing them
over her shoulder, and march away.   " We
wished," says this lady, " that our mothers
would let us have hooded cloaks, that we might
carry our books in the same way."

It is known that Margaret had several love
affairs and, in a later letter, she refers to one
which belongs to this period, and which appears
to have been the first of the series.   She meets
her old adorer again at the age of thirty and
writes to a friend who knew of the youthful
episode.   He had the same powerful eye, calm
wisdom, refined observation and " the imposing

maniere d' etre which anywhere would give him influence among men"; but in herself, she says, " There is scarcely a fibre left of the haughty, passionate, ambitious child he remembered and loved."

Though a precocious girl and in a way fascinating, there is evidence that Margaret was crude and unformed socially, due perhaps to the habit of considering her mother as a negligible quantity. Cambridge ladies preserved an unpleasant portrait of the child as she appeared at a grand reception given by Mr. Fuller to President Adams in 1826, " one of the most elaborate affairs of the kind," says Col. Higginson, " that had occurred in Cambridge since the ante-revolutionary days of the Lechmeres and Vassals." Margaret ought to have been dressed by an artist, but apparently, a girl of sixteen, she was left to her own devices. She appeared, we are told, with a low-necked dress badly cut, tightly laced, her arms held back as if pinioned, her hair curled all over her head, and she danced quadrilles very badly. This escapade was not allowed to repeat itself. Certain kind and motherly Cambridge ladies took the neglected child in hand, tamed her rude strength, and subdued her manners. Col. Higginson mentions half a dozen of these excellent ladies, among them his mother, at whose feet " this studious, self-conscious, overgrown girl " would sit, " covering her hands with kisses and treasuring every word."

Chief among Margaret's motherly friends was Mrs. Eliza Farrar, wife of a Harvard professor, an authoress of merit, " of uncommon character and cultivation, who had lived much in Europe, and who, with no children of her own," became a kind of foster-mother to Margaret. She had Margaret " constantly at her own house, reformed her hairdresser, instructed her dressmaker, and took her to make calls and on journeys." Margaret was an apt pupil, and the good training of these many Cambridge mothers was apparent when, ten years later, Mr. Emerson made her acquaintance. " She was then, as always," he says, " carefully and becomingly dressed, and of lady-like self-possession."

The seven years in Cambridge, from Margaret's fifteenth to her twenty-third year, though uneventful, were, considering merely the pleasure of existence, the most delightful of her life. She was a school-girl as much or as little as she cared to be; her health, when not overtaxed, was perfect; her family though not rich, were in easy circumstances; her father was distinguished, having just retired from Congress after eight years of creditable service; and, partly perhaps from her father's distinction, she had access to the best social circles of Cambridge. "In our evening reunions," says Dr. Hedge, "she was always conspicuous by the brilliancy of her wit, which needed but little provocation to break forth in exuberant sallies, that drew around her a knot of listeners, and made her the central attraction of the hour. Rarely did she enter a company in which she was not a prominent object." Her conversational talent "continued to develop itself in these years, and was certainly" he thinks, "her most decided gift. One could form no adequate idea of her ability without hearing her converse. . . . For some reason or other, she could never deliver herself in print as she did with her lips." Emerson, in perfect agreement with this estimate says, "Her pen was a non-conductor." The reader will not think this true in her letters, where often the words seem to palpitate. Doubtless the world had no business to see her love letters, but one will find there a woman who, if she could speak as she writes, must have poured herself out in tidal waves.

Dr. Hedge was struck by two traits of Margaret's character, repeatedly mentioned by others, but to which it is worth while to have his testimony. The first was a passionate love for the beautiful: " I have never known one who seemed to derive such satisfaction from beautiful forms "; the second was " her intellectual sincerity. Her judgment took no bribes from her sex or her sphere, nor from custom, nor tradition, nor caprice."

Margaret was nineteen years old when Dr. James Freeman Clarke, then a young man in college, made her acquaintance. " We both lived in Cambridge," he says, " and from that time until she went to reside in Groton in 1833, I saw her or heard from her almost every day. There was a family connection between us, and we called each other cousins." Possessing in a greater degree than any person he ever knew, the power of magnetizing others, she had drawn about her a circle of girl friends whom she entertained and delighted by her exuberant talent. They came from Boston, Charlestown, Roxbury, Brookline, and met now at one house and now at another of these pleasant towns.

Dr. Hedge also knows of this charming circle, and says, " she loved to draw these fair girls to herself, and make them her guests, and was never so happy as when surrounded in company by such a bevy."

With all her social activity, Margaret kept up her studies at a rate that would be the despair of a young man in college. " She already, when I first became acquainted with her," says Dr. Clarke, " had become familiar with the masterpieces of French, Italian, and Spanish literature," and was beginning German, and in about three months, she was reading with ease the masterpieces of German literature. Meanwhile, she was keeping up her Greek as a pastime, reading over and over the dialogues of Plato. Still there is time for Mr. Clarke to walk with her for hours beneath the lindens or in the garden, or, on a summer's day to ride with her on horseback from Cambridge to Newton,— a day he says, " all of a piece, in which my eloquent companion helped me to understand my past life and her own."

We cannot wonder that, at the age of twenty-three, Margaret reluctantly left Cambridge where there was so much that she loved, and went with her family to a farm in Groton where,

[181]

with certain unpleasant school-girl memories, there was nothing that she loved at all. In 1833, at the age of sixty-five Mr. Fuller retired from his law practice and bought an estate in Groton, with the double purpose of farming his lands for income, and, in his leisure, writing a history of the United States, for which his public life had been a preparation, and towards which he had collected much material. Margaret's most exacting duties were the education of the younger children, which left her much time for her favorite studies. She had correspondents by the score; her friends visited her; Cambridge homes were open to her; and Mrs. Farrar took her on a delightful journey to Newport, Hudson River and Trenton Falls. Still we cannot add the two years in Groton to her happy period, because she allowed herself to be intensely miserable. Six years later, in a moment of penitence, she said of this period, " Had I been wise in such matters then as now, how easy and fair I might have made the whole."

She fought her homesickness by overwork, so that Emerson says, " her reading in Groton was at a rate like Gibbon's," and she paid the penalty of her excesses by a serious illness which threatened to be fatal, and from which perhaps she never fully recovered. It was some consolation that her father was melted to an unwonted exhibition of tenderness, and that he said to her in this mood, " My dear, I have been thinking of you in the night, and I cannot remember that you have any faults. You have defects, of course, as all mortals have, but I do not know that you have a single fault."

Events were soon to make this remark one of her dearest memories. In a short time, death separated the father and child, who had been so much to each other. In 1835, Mr. Fuller fell a victim to cholera, and died in three days. For a year or more, Margaret's heart had been set upon a visit to Europe for study; the trip had been promised by her father; it had been arranged that she should accompany her friends, the Farrars; but the death of Mr. Fuller dissolved this dream, and, in her journal, solemnly praying that " duty may now be the first object and self set aside," she dedicates her strength to her " mother, brothers, and sister." No one can read the " Memoirs " without feeling that she kept her vows.

The estate of Mr. Fuller finally yielded $2,000 to each of the seven children, much less, Margaret says, than was anticipated. With reason, she wrote, " Life, as I look forward, presents a scene of struggle and privation only." In the winter, at Mrs. Farrar's, Margaret met Mr. Emerson; the summer following she visited at his house in Concord. There she met Mr. Alcott and engaged to teach in his school in Boston.

Margaret Fuller's visit at Mr. Emerson's in 1836 had for her very important consequences. It was the first of many visits and was the beginning of an intimacy which takes its place among the most interesting literary friendships in the history of letters. To this friendship Col. Higginson devotes a separate chapter in his biography of Margaret, and in the " Memoirs," under the title of " Visits to Concord," Mr. Emerson gives a charming account of it in more than a hundred pages.

Mr. Emerson was by no means the stranger to Margaret that she was to him. She had sat under his preaching during his pastorate at the Second Church in Boston, and " several of his sermons," so she wrote to a friend, " stood apart in her memory like landmarks in her spiritual history." It appears that she had failed to come to close quarters with this timid apostle. A year after he left his pulpit, she wrote of him

as the " only clergyman of all possible clergy-
men who eludes my acquaintance."

When, at length, she was invited to Concord,
it was as Mrs. Emerson's guest, not as his: " she
came to spend a fortnight with my wife."
However, at last she was under his roof. " I
still remember," he says, " the first half hour of
her conversation. . . . Her extreme plainness,— a trick of incessantly opening and shut-
ting her eyelids,— the nasal tone of her voice —
all repelled; and I said to myself, we shall never
get far. . . . I remember that she made
me laugh more than I liked. . . . She had
an incredible variety of anecdotes, and the read-
iest wit to give an absurd turn to whatever
passed; and the eyes, which were so plain at first,
soon swam with fun and drolleries, and the very
tides of joy and superabundant life."

The practical outcome of the visit was an engagement to teach in Mr. Alcott's school.
Under date of August 2, 1836, Mr. Alcott
writes, " Emerson called this morning and took
me to Concord to spend the day. At his house,
I met Margaret Fuller. . . . and had some
conversation with her about taking Miss Peabody's place in my school." That is to say, Mr.
Emerson had in his house a brilliant young lady

who, by stress of circumstances, wanted a situation; he had a friend in Boston in whose school there was a vacancy; Mr. Emerson, at some pains to himself, brought the parties together. Nor was this the last time that Mr. Emerson befriended Margaret.

It appears from Mr. Alcott's diary that Miss Fuller began her engagement with January, that she taught Latin and French at the school, and French, German, and Italian to private classes. For a class of beginners, she " thought it good success," she says, " when at the end of three months, they could read twenty pages of German at a lesson, and very well." An advanced class in German read Goethe's Hermann and Dorothea, Goetz von Berlichingen, Iphigenia, and the first part of Faust, " three weeks of thorough study," she calls it, " as valuable to me as to them."

The class in Italian went at an equal pace. At the same time she had three private pupils, to one of whom, every day for ten weeks, she taught Latin " orally,"— in other words, Latin conversation. In her leisure, she " translated, one evening every week, German authors into English for the gratification of Dr. Channing." It is to be hoped that she was paid for this

[186]

service, because she found it far from interesting. "It is not very pleasant," she writes, "for Dr. Channing takes in subjects more deliberately than is conceivable to us feminine people."

In the spring of 1837, Margaret accepted an invitation to teach in a private academy in Providence, R.I.— four hours a day, at a salary of $1,000. We are not told how this invitation came to her, but it is not difficult to detect the hand of Mr. Emerson. The proprietor of the school was an admirer of Emerson, so much so that he brought Emerson from Concord in June following, to dedicate a new school building. His relation to both parties makes it probable that Margaret owed her second engagement, as she did her first, to the good offices of Mr. Emerson.

She taught in this school with success, two years, "worshipped by the girls," it is said, "but sometimes too sarcastic for the boys." The task of teaching, however, was irksome to her, her mind was in literature; she had from Mr. Ripley a definite proposition to write a "Life of Goethe," a task of which she had dreamed many years; and she resigned her position, and withdrew from the profession of school-teacher, at the end of 1838. Her life of Goethe was never written, but it was always dancing before her eyes and, more than once, determined her course.

In the following spring, Margaret took a pleasant house in Jamaica Plain, "then and perhaps now," Col. Higginson says, "the most rural and attractive suburb of Boston." Here she brought her mother and the younger children. Three years later, she removed with them to Cambridge, and for the next five years, she kept the family together, and made a home for them. In addition to the income of the estate, she expected to meet her expenses by giving lessons. Two pupils came with her from Providence, and other pupils came for recitations, by whom she was paid at the rate of two dollars an hour.

With these resources the life in Jamaica Plain began very quietly and pleasantly. To be quiet however was not natural to Margaret. Besides, she had fallen upon what, intellectually, were stirring times. It was at the high tide of the Transcendental movement. William Henry Channing who, like Margaret, was a part of it, says, "the summer of 1839 saw the full dawn of this strange enthusiasm." As he briefly defines

it " Transcendentalism, as viewed by its disciples, was a pilgrimage from the idolatrous world
of creeds and rituals to the temple of the living
God in the soul." Its disciples, says Mr. Channing, " were pleasantly nick-named the ' Like-
minded,' on the ground that no two were of the
same opinion." Of this company, he says,
" Margaret was a member by the grace of
nature. . . . Men, her superiors in years,
in fame and social position, treated her more
with the frankness due from equal to equal, than
the half condescending deference with which
scholars are wont to adapt themselves to women.
. . . It was evident that they prized her
verdict, respected her criticism, feared her re-
buke, and looked to her as an umpire." In
speaking, " her opening was deliberate, like the
progress of a massive force gaining its momen-
tum; but as she felt her way, and moving in a
congenial element, the sweep of her speech became grand. The style of her eloquence was
sententious, free from prettiness, direct, vigorous, charged with vitality."

It was a saying of hers that if she had been a
man, she would have aspired to become an orator,
and it seems probable she would not have aspired
in vain. The natural sequel to the occasional

discussions of the summer was the formation of a class of ladies for Conversation, with Margaret as the leader. This class contained twenty-five or thirty ladies, among whom were Mrs. George Bancroft, Mrs. Lydia Maria Child, Mrs. Horace Mann, Mrs. Theodore Parker, Mrs. Waldo Emerson, Mrs. George Ripley, and Mrs. Josiah Quincy. The first series of thirteen meetings was immediately followed by a second series; they were resumed the next winter and were continued with unabated interest for five years.

The subjects considered in these celebrated Conversations ranged over a very wide field, from mythology and religion, poetry and art, to war, ethics, and sociology. If Margaret had not been brilliant in these assemblies, she would have fallen short of herself as she has been represented in the Cambridge drawing-rooms. As reported by one of the members of the class, " Margaret used to come to the conversations very well dressed and, altogether, looked sumptuously. She began them with an exordium in which she gave her leading views,"— a part which she is further said to have managed with great skill and charm, after which she invited others to join in the discussion. Mr. Emerson tells us that the apparent sumptuousness in her attire was imaginary, the "effect of a general impression made by her genius and mistakenly attributed to some external elegance; for," he says, "I have been told by her most intimate friend, who knew every particular of her conduct at the time, that there was nothing of especial expense or splendor in her toilette."

Mr. Emerson knew a lady "of eminent powers, previously by no means partial to Margaret," who said, on leaving one of these assemblies, "I never heard, read of, or imagined a conversation at all equal to this we have now heard." Many testimonies have been brought together, in the "Memoirs," of the enthusiasm and admiration created by Margaret in these Conversations. They were probably her most brilliant achievements, though, in the nature of the case, nothing survives of them but the echo in these recorded memories of participants.

Mr. Emerson says that "the fame of these conversations" led to a proposal that Margaret should undertake an evening class to which gentlemen should be admitted and that he himself had the pleasure of "assisting at one — the second — of these soirees." Margaret "spoke well — she could not otherwise,— but I remember that she seemed encumbered, or interrupted, by the headiness or incapacity of the men." A lady who attended the entire series, a "true hand," he says, reports that "all that depended on others entirely failed" and that "even in the point of erudition, which Margaret did not profess on the subject, she proved the best informed of the party." This testimony is worth something in answer to the charge that Margaret's scholarship was fictitious, that she had a smattering of many things, but knew nothing thoroughly. She seems to have compared well with others, some of whom were considered scholars. "Take her as a whole," said Mr. Emerson's informant, "she has the most to bestow on others by conversation of any person I have ever known."

For these services, Margaret seems to have received liberal compensation, though all was so cordial that she says she never had the feeling of being "a paid Corinne." For the conversations with ladies and gentlemen, according to Mrs. Dall who has published her notes of them, the tickets were $20 each, for the series of ten evenings.

It appears from his account that Mr. Emerson saw much of Margaret during these years and that she was frequently his guest. "The day," he says, " was never long enough to exhaust her opulent memory; and I, who knew her intimately for ten years,— from July, 1836, till August, 1846, when she sailed for Europe,— never saw her without a surprise at her new powers." She was as busy as he, and they seldom met in the forenoon, but " In the evening, she came to the library, and many and many a conversation was there held," he tells us, " whose details, if they could be preserved, would justify all encomiums. They interested me in every manner; — talent, memory, wit, stern introspection, poetic play, religion, the finest personal feeling, the aspects of the future, each followed each in full activity, and left me, I remember, enriched, and sometimes astonished by the gifts of my guest."

She was " rich in friends," and wore them " as a necklace of diamonds about her neck." " She was an active and inspiring companion and correspondent, and all the art, the thought and nobleness of New England seemed, at that moment, related to her and she to it. She was everywhere a welcome guest. . . . Her arrival was a holiday, and so was her abode. . . . all tasks that could be suspended were put aside to catch the favorable hour, in walking, riding, or boating to talk with this joyful guest, who brought wit, anecdotes, love-stories, tragedies, oracles with her, and, with her broad relations to so many fine friends, seemed like the queen of some parliament of love, who carried the key to all confidences, and to whom every question had been finally referred."

At a later day, when Margaret was in Italy, reports came back that she was making conquests, and having advantageous offers of marriage. Even Mr. Emerson expressed surprise at these social successes in a strange land, but a lady said to him, "There is nothing extraordinary in it. Had she been a man, any one of those fine girls of sixteen, who surrounded her here, would have married her: they were all in love with her."

"Of personal influence, speaking strictly,— an efflux, that is, purely of mind and character," Mr. Emerson thinks she had more than any other person he ever knew. Even a recluse like Hawthorne yielded to this influence. Hawthorne was married to Miss Sophia Peabody in 1842, and began housekeeping in the Old Manse in Concord. The day following their engagement Miss Peabody wrote Miss Fuller addressing her "Dear, most noble Margaret," and saying, "I feel that you are entitled, through our love and regard to be told directly. . . . Mr. Hawthorne, last evening, in the midst of his emotions, so deep and absorbing, after deciding, said that Margaret can now, when she visits Mr. Emerson spend part of the time with us." A month after the marriage, Hawthorne himself wrote to Margaret, "There is nobody to whom I would more willingly speak my mind, because I can be certain of being understood." Evidently he is not beginning an acquaintance; he already knows Margaret intimately and respects her thoroughly. There is no evidence, I believe, that during her life, he held any different opinion of her.

These facts have become of special interest because, in Italy, eight years after her death, he wrote in his Note-Book, that Margaret "had a strong and coarse nature" and that "she was a great humbug." The most reasonable explanation of this change of view is that Margaret was dead, poor woman, and could not speak for herself; that she had fought with all her might in an Italian Revolution that had failed; that having failed, she and her party were discredited; that her enemies survived, and Hawthorne listened to them. However his later opinions may be explained, the quality of her friends in America, among whom had been Hawthorne himself, is evidence that Margaret was not of a " coarse nature," and it is incredible that a " humbug " could have imposed herself for five years upon those ladies who attended her conversations, not to speak of James Freeman Clarke who was a fair scholar and Dr. Hedge who was a very rare scholar.

Margaret had her weaknesses, which her friends do not conceal. It was a weakness, not perhaps that she overestimated herself; that might be pardoned; but that she took no pains to conceal her high opinion of her abilities and worth. One likes to see an appearance of modesty, and that little deceit Margaret did not practice. On the contrary, Mr. Emerson says, " Margaret at first astonished and then repelled us by a complacency that seemed the most assured since the days of Scaligar. . . . In the coolest way, she said to her friends, ' I now know all the people worth knowing in America, and I find no intellect comparable to my own.' . . . It is certain that Margaret occasionally let slip, with all the innocence imaginable, some phrase betraying the presence of a rather mountainous ME, in a way to surprise those who knew her good sense." Col. Higginson quotes a saying about the Fullers, that " Their only peculiarity was that they said openly about themselves the good and bad things which we commonly suppress about ourselves and express only about other people." The common way is not more sincere, but it is pleasanter.

In 1840, the second year of Margaret's Conversations, appeared the first number of *The Dial*, a literary magazine of limited circulation, but destined to a kind of post-mortem immortality. In 1841, the Community of Brook Farm was established. An interesting account of both enterprises, and of Margaret's part in them, is given by Mr. Emerson in a paper found in the tenth volume of his collected Works. In the preliminary discussions leading to both enterprises, Margaret participated. Like Mr. Emerson, she did not have unqualified faith in the Brook Farm experiment and did not join the community, though she had many friends in it, was a frequent visitor, and had the honor to sit for the portrait of " Zenobia " in Mr. Hawthorne's Blithedale Romance.

Her part in *The Dial* was more prominent. She edited the first two volumes of the magazine, being then succeeded by Mr. Emerson, and she wrote for it a paper entitled " Man vs. Men: Woman vs. Women," afterward expanded and published in a volume under the title, " Woman in the Nineteenth Century," her second and most famous book. Her first book, " Summer on the Lakes," is an account of a charming journey, with the family of James Freeman Clarke and others, by steamboat and farm wagon, as far as the Mississippi. It was a voyage of discovery, and her account has permanent historic interest.

In 1844, Margaret accepted an advantageous offer to become literary editor of the *New York Tribune*, a position which she was admirably qualified to fill. A collection of papers from *The Tribune*, under the title of " Literature and Art," made up her third book, published in 1846, on the eve of her departure for Europe.

During her residence in New York, she became greatly interested in philanthropies, especially in the care of prisoners of her own sex. She visited the jails and prisons, interviewed the inmates, gave them " conversations," and wrought upon them the same miracle which she had so often performed in refined drawing-rooms. " If she had been born to large fortune," said Mr. Greeley, " a house of refuge for all female outcasts desiring to return to the ways of virtue

would have been one of her most cherished and
and first realized conceptions."

Early in her New York residence must also
have occurred that rather mysterious love affair
with the young Hebrew, Mr. Nathan, who seems
first to have charmed her with his music and then
with his heart. After nearly sixty years, the
letters which she wrote him, full of consuming
fire, have at last seen the light. From a passage
in one of them, it would seem that marriage was
not contemplated by either party, that in theory
at least they took no thought of the morrow, the
bliss of the moment being held sufficient. Evidently there was no engagement, but no one can
doubt that on her part there was love. Of
course in this changing world, no such relations
can be maintained for ever, and in the end there
will be an awakening, and then pain..

In 1846, Margaret realized her life-dream and
went to Europe. Destined to a life of adventure, she was accidently separated from her
party, and spent a perilous night on Ben
Lomond, without a particle of shelter, in a
drenching rain, a thrilling account of which she
has written. She visited Carlyle and, for a
wonder, he let her take a share in the conversation. To Mr. Emerson he wrote, Margaret " is

very narrow sometimes, but she is truly high."

On her way to Italy, the goal of her ambition, she visited George Sand and they had such a meeting as two women of genius might. She sailed from Genoa for Naples in February, 1847, and arrived in Rome in May following. There is much to interest a reader in her Italian life, but the one thing which cannot be omitted is the story of her marriage to the Marquis Ossoli. Soon after her arrival in Rome, on a visit to St. Peter's, Margaret became separated from her friends, whom she did not again discover at the place appointed for meeting. A gentleman seeing her distress, offered to get her a carriage and, not finding one, walked home with her. This was the young Marquis Ossoli, and thus fortuitously the acquaintance began, which was continued by occasional meetings. The summer Margaret spent in the north of Italy, and when she returned to Rome, she took modest apartments in which she received her friends every Monday evening, and the Marquis came very regularly.

It was not long however before he confessed his love for her and asked her hand in marriage. He was gently rejected, being told that he ought to marry a younger woman, and that she would be his friend but not his wife. He however persisted, at length won her consent, and they were privately married in December. I follow the account of Mrs. William Story, wife of the artist, then residing in Rome. The old Marquis Ossoli had recently died, leaving an unsettled estate, of which his two older sons, both in the Papal service, were the executors. "Every one knows," says Mrs. Story, "that law is subject to ecclesiastical influence in Rome, and that marriage with a Protestant would be destructive of all prospect of favorable administration."

The birth of a child a year later, at Rieti in the Appenines, whither Margaret had retired, made secrecy seem more imperative; or, as Margaret said, in order to defend the child "from the stings of poverty, they were patient waiters for the restored law of the land." The Italian Revolution of 1848 was then in progress. Ossoli her husband, was a captain in the Civic Guard, on duty in Rome, and the letters which she wrote him at this period of trial, were the only fragments of her treasures recovered from the wreck in which she perished.

Leaving her babe with his nurse, in April following, she visited Rome and was shut up in the siege by the French army which had been sent to overthrow the provisional government and restore the authority of the pope. " Ossoli took station with his men on the walls of the Vatican garden where he remained faithfully to the end of the attack. Margaret had entire charge of one of the hospitals. . . . I have walked through the wards with her," says Mrs. Story, " and seen how comforting was her presence to the poor suffering men. ' How long will the Signora stay?' ' When will the Signora come again?' they eagerly asked. . . . They raised themselves up on their elbows to get the last glimpse of her as she was going away."

In the midst of these dangers, Margaret confided to Mrs. Story the secret of her marriage and placed in her hands the marriage certificate and other documents relating to the affair. These papers were afterward returned to Margaret and were lost in the wreck.

The failure of the Revolution was the financial ruin of all those who had staked their fortunes in it. They had much reason to be thankful if they escaped with their lives. By the intervention of friends, the Ossolis were dealt with very leniently. Mr. Greenough, the artist, interested himself in their behalf and procured for them permission to retire, outside the papal territory,

to Florence. Ossoli even obtained a small part
of his patrimony.

Except the disappointment and sorrow over
the faded dream of Italian Independence, the
winter at Florence was one of the bright spots in
Margaret's life. She was proud of her husband's part in the Revolution: " I rejoice," she
says, " in all Ossoli did." She had her babe
with her and her happiness in husband and child
was perfect: " My love for Ossoli is most pure
and tender, nor has any one, except my mother
or little children, loved me so genuinely as he
does. . . . Ossoli seems to me more lovely
and good every day; our darling child is well
now, and every day more gay and playful."

She found pleasant and congenial society: " I
see the Brownings often," she says, " and love
them both more and more as I know them better.
Mr. Browning enriches every hour I spend with
him, and is a most cordial, true, and noble man.
One of my most prized Italian friends, Mar-
chioness Arconati Visconti, of Milan, is passing
the winter here, and I see her almost every day."
Moreover she was busy with a congenial task.
At the very opening of the struggle for liberty,
she planned to write a history of the eventful
period, and with this purpose, collected material

for the undertaking, and already had a large part of the work in manuscript. She finished the writing in Florence, and much value was set upon it both by herself and by her friends in Italy. Mrs. Story says, " in the estimation of most of those who were in Italy at the time, the loss of Margaret's history and notes is a great and irreparable one. No one could have possessed so many avenues of direct information from both sides."

When the spring opened, it was decided to return to America, partly to negotiate directly with the publisher, but chiefly because, having exhausted her resources, Margaret's pen must henceforth be the main reliance of the little family. It is pathetic to know that, after their passage had been engaged, " letters came which, had they reached her a week earlier, would probably have induced them to remain in Italy."

They sailed, May 17, 1850, in a merchant vessel, the only other passengers being the baby's nurse and Mr. Horace Sumner, a younger brother of Senator Sumner. After a protracted and troubled voyage of two months, the vessel arrived off the coast of New Jersey, on July 18. The " weather was thick. . . . By nine p. m. there was a gale, by midnight a hurri-

cane," and at four o'clock on the morning of
July 19, the vessel grounded on the shallow
sands of Fire Island. The captain had died of
smallpox on the voyage; his widow, the mate in
command of the vessel, and four seamen reached
the shore; Mr. Sumner and the Ossolis perished.
The cruel part of the tragedy is that it seems
probable every soul on board might have been
saved. Life-boats, only three miles away, did
not arrive until noon; that is, after eight
precious hours had passed. Moreover, in a
moment of penitence, one of the life-boat crew
said, " Oh, if we had known that any such persons of importance were on board, we should
have done our best."

Margaret, the name by which she will always
be known, had passed her fortieth birthday at
sea on this voyage. It seems a short life in
which to have crowded so much and such varied
experience. She had some trials even in her
youth, but for two-thirds of her existence, she
might have been considered a favorite of fortune. In later life, she had some battles to
fight, but her triumphs were great enough to
dazzle a person with more modesty than was her
endowment. She suffered in Italy, both for her
child left to strangers in the mountains, and for

her adopted country, but they were both causes, in which for her, suffering was a joy. She did not desire to survive her husband and child, nor to leave them behind, and, we may say, happily they all went together. "Her life seems to me," says Col. Higginson, "on the whole, a triumphant rather than a sad one," and that is a reasonable verdict, however difficult to render in the presence of such a tragedy as her untimely death.

VI
HARRIET BEECHER STOWE

HARRIET BEECHER STOWE

"Is this the little woman who made this great war!" exclaimed President Lincoln when, in 1862, Mrs. Stowe was introduced to him. There was but one woman in America to whom this could have been said without absurdity. "Uncle Tom's Cabin" was so conspicuous a factor in bringing on the war which abolished American slavery that to credit these results to Mrs. Stowe was not fulsome flattery but graceful compliment.

There are two excellent biographies of Mrs. Stowe, one published in 1889, by her son, Rev. Charles E. Stowe, and one, in 1897, by Mrs. Annie Fields. That work will hardly need to be done again. The object of this sketch is to study the influences that moulded Mrs. Stowe, to present the salient features of her career, and, incidentally, to discover her characteristic qualities. Her fame rests upon her literary achievements, and these are comparatively well known. Her literary career can hardly be said to have begun until the age of forty and, if this were

[209]

the only interest her life had for us, we could pass hastily over her youth. It will be found however that her religious development, begun prematurely with her fourth year and continued without consideration or discretion until at seventeen she became a chronic invalid, gives a kind of tragic interest to her earlier years. Her religious education may not have been unique; it may have been characteristic of much of the religious life of New England, but girls set at work upon the problems of their souls at the age of four have seldom attained the distinction of having their biographies written, so that one can study their history.

Harriet, the second daughter and seventh child of Lyman Beecher and Roxanna Foote, was born in Litchfield, Conn., June 14, 1811. There were three Mrs. Lyman Beechers of whom Roxanna Foote was the first. The Footes were Episcopalians, Harriet, sister of Roxanna, being as Mrs. Stowe says, " the highest of High Churchwomen who in her private heart did not consider my father an ordained minister." Roxanna, perhaps not so high-church, held out for two years against Dr. Beecher's assaults upon her heart and then consented to become his wife.

HARRIET BEECHER STOWE

Mrs. Beecher was a refined and cultivated lady who "read all the new works that were published at that day," numbered painting among her accomplishments, and whose house "was full of little works of ingenuity and taste and skill, which had been wrought by her hand: pictures of birds and flowers, done with minutest skill"; but her greatest charm was a religious nature full of all gentleness and sweetness. "In no exigency," says Dr. Beecher, "was she taken by surprise. She was just there, quiet as an angel above." There seems to have been but one thing which this saintly woman with an Episcopalian education could not do to meet the expectations of a Congregational parish, and that was that "in the weekly female prayer-meeting she could never lead the devotions"; but from this duty she seems to have been excused because of her known sensitiveness and timidity.

Mrs. Beecher died when Harriet was in her fourth year, but she left an indelible impression upon her family. Her "memory met us everywhere," says Mrs. Stowe; "when father wished to make an appeal to our hearts which he knew we could not resist, he spoke of mother." It had been the mother's prayer that her sons, of whom there were six, should be ministers, and ministers they all were. One incident Mrs. Stowe remembered which may be supposed to have set Sunday apart as a day of exceptional sanctity. It was that " of our all running and dancing out before her from the nursery to the sitting-room one Sabbath morning and her pleasant voice saying after us, ' Remember the Sabbath day to keep it holy.' " Such early religious impressions made upon the mind of a child of four would have faded in other surroundings, but it will be seen that Harriet's environment gave no rest to her little soul.

After the death of her mother, the child was sent to her grandmother Foote's for a long visit. There she fell to the charge of her aunt Harriet, than whom, we are told, " a more energetic human being never undertook the education of a child." According to her views, " little girls were to be taught to move very gently, to speak softly and prettily, to say ' Yes ma 'am ' and ' No ma 'am,' never to tear their clothes, to sew and knit at regular hours, to go to church on Sunday and make all the responses, and to come home and be catechised. I remember those catechisings when she used to place my little cousin Mary and myself bolt upright at her knee while black Dinah and Harvey, the bound boy, were ranged at a respectful distance behind us. . . . I became a proficient in the Church catechism and gave my aunt great satisfaction by the old-fashioned gravity and steadiness with which I learned to repeat it." This early training in the catechism and the responses bore fruit in giving Mrs. Stowe a life-long fondness for the Episcopal service and ultimately in taking her into the Episcopal Church, of which during her last thirty years she was a communicant. Harriet signalized her fifth year by committing to memory twenty-seven hymns and " two long chapters of the Bible," and even more perhaps, by accidentally discovering in the attic a discarded volume of the " Arabian Nights," with which, she says, her fortune was made. It was a much more suitable child's book, one would think, than the Church catechism or Watts's hymns.

At the age of six Harriet passed to the care of the second Mrs. Lyman Beecher, formerly Harriet Porter, of Portland, Maine, apparently a lady of great dignity and character. " We felt," says Mrs. Stowe, " a little in awe of her, as if she were a strange princess rather than our own mamma; but her voice was very sweet, her ways of speaking and moving very graceful, and she took us up in her lap and let us play with her beautiful hands which seemed wonderful things, made of pearl and ornamented with strange rings." It appears she was a faithful mother, though a little severe and repressive. Henry Ward Beecher said of her: " She did the office-work of a mother if ever a mother did "; she " performed to the uttermost her duties, according to her ability "; she " was a woman of profound veneration rather than of a warm loving nature. Therefore her prayer was invariably a prayer of deep yearning reverence. I remember well the impression which it made on me. There was a mystic influence about it. A sort of sympathetic hold it had on me, but still I always felt when I went to prayer, as though I were going into a crypt, where the sun was not allowed to come; and I shrunk from it." To complete the portrait of this conscientious lady who was to have the supervision of Harriet from her sixth year, the following from a letter of one of the Beecher children is worth quoting: " Mamma is well and don't laugh any more than she did." Evidently a rather stern and sobering influence had come into the Beecher family.

" In her religion," says Mrs. Stowe, " she was distinguished by a most unfaltering Christ-worship. . . . Had it not been that Dr. Payson had set up and kept before her a tender, human, loving Christ, she would have been only a conscientious bigot. This image, however, gave softness and warmth to her religious life, and I have since noticed how her Christ-enthusiasm has sprung up in the hearts of all her children." This passage is of peculiar interest as it shows the source of what Mrs. Stowe loves to call the " Christ-worship " which characterized the religion of the younger Beechers. Writing at the age of seventeen, when her soul was tossing between Scylla and Charybdis, Harriet says: " I feel that I love God,— that is, that I love Christ "; and in 1876, writing of her brother Henry, she says, " He and I are Christ-worshippers, adoring him as the Image of the Invisible God." Her son refers us to the twenty-fourth chapter of the Minister's Wooing for a complete presentation of this subject " of Christ-worship." Mrs. Stowe speaks of this belief as a plain departure from ordinary Trinitarianism, as a kind of heresy which it has required some courage to hold. The heresy seems to have consisted in practically dropping the first and third persons in the Godhead and accepting Christ as the only God we know or need to consider.

As Mrs. Stowe during her adult life was an invalid, it is interesting to have Mrs. Beecher's testimony that, on her arrival, she was met by a lovely family of children and " with heartfelt gratitude," she says, " I observed how cheerful and healthy they were."   When Harriet was ten years of age, she began to attend the Litchfield Academy and was recognized as one of its brightest pupils. She especially excelled in writing compositions and, at the age of twelve, her essay was one of two or three selected to be read at a school exhibition. After Harriet's had been read, Dr. Beecher turned to the teacher and asked, " Who wrote that composition?" " Your daughter, Sir," was the reply. " It was," says Mrs. Stowe, " the proudest moment of my life."

" Can the immortality of the soul be proved by the light of Nature?" was the subject of this juvenile composition, a strange choice for a girl of twelve summers; but in this family the religious climate was tropical, and forced development.   As might have been expected, she easily proved that nothing of immortality could be known by the light of nature.   She had been too well instructed to think otherwise. Dr. Beecher himself had no good opinion of 'the light of nature.' "They say," said he, "that everybody knows about God naturally. A lie. All such ideas are by teaching." If Harriet had taken the other side of her question and argued as every believer tries to to-day, she would have deserved some credit for originality. Nevertheless the form of her argument is remarkable for her years, and would not have dishonored Dr. Beecher's next sermon. This amazing achievement of a girl of twelve can be read in the Life of Mrs. Stowe by her son.

From the Litchfield Academy, Harriet was sent to the celebrated Female Seminary established by her sister Catharine at Hartford, Conn. She here began the study of Latin and, " at the end of the first year, made a translation of Ovid in verse which was read at the final exhibition of the school." It was her ambition to be a poet and she began a play called ' Cleon,' filling " blank book after blank book with this drama." Mrs. Fields prints six pages of this poem and the specimens have more than enough merit to convince one that the author might have attained distinction as a poet. Her energetic sister Catharine however put an end to this innocent diversion, saying that she must not waste her time writing poetry but discipline her mind upon Butler's Analogy. To enforce compliance, Harriet was assigned to teach the Analogy to a class of girls as old as herself, " being compelled to master each chapter just ahead of the class." This occupation, with Latin, French and Italian, sufficiently protected her from the dissipation of writing poetry.

Harriet remained in the Hartford school, as pupil and teacher, from her thirteenth to her twenty-third year. In her spiritual history, this was an important period. It may seem that her soul had hitherto not been neglected but as yet youth and a sunny nature had kept her from any agonies of Christian experience. Now her time had come. No one under the care of the stern Puritan, Catharine Beecher, would be suffered to forget her eternal interests. Both of Mrs. Stowe's biographers feel the necessity of making us acquainted with this masterful lady, " whose strong, vigorous mind and tremendous personality," says Mr. Stowe, " indelibly stamped themselves on the sensitive, dreamy, poetic nature of her younger sister."

It was Catharine's distinction to have written, it is claimed, the best refutation of Edwards on the Will ever published. She was undoubtedly the most acute and vigorous intellect in the Beecher family. Like all the members of her remarkable family, she was intensely religious and, at the period when Harriet passed to her care, gloomily religious. It could not have been otherwise. She had been engaged to marry Prof. Alexander Fisher, of Yale College, a young man of great promise. Unhappily, he was drowned at sea, and she believed his soul was eternally lost. It is futile to ask why Yale College should have entrusted a professorship to a man whom the Lord would send to perdition, or why Miss Beecher should have loved such an abandoned character; it is enough to say that she loved him and that she believed his soul to be lost; and was it her fault that she could not be a cheerful companion to a young girl of thirteen?

As we have seen, Harriet must not fritter away her time writing plays; she must study Butler's Analogy. She must also read Baxter's Saints Rest, than which, says Mrs. Stowe, " no book ever affected me more powerfully. As I walked the pavements I wished that they might sink beneath me if only I might find myself in heaven." In this mental condition she went to her home in Litchfield to spend her vacation. One dewy fresh Sunday morning of that period stood by itself in her memory. "I knew," she says, "it was sacramental Sunday, and thought with sadness that when all the good people should take the bread and wine I should be left out. I tried hard to think of my sins and count them up; but what with the birds, the daisies, and the brooks that rippled by the way, it was impossible." The sermon of Dr. Beecher was unusually sweet and tender and when he appealed to his hearers to trust themselves to Jesus, their faithful friend, she says, "I longed to cry out I will. Then the awful thought came over me that I had never had any conviction of my sins and consequently could not come to him." Happily the inspiration came to her that if she needed conviction of sin and Jesus were such a friend, he would give it to her; she would trust him for the whole, and she went home illumined with joy.

When her father returned, she fell into his arms saying, "Father, I have given myself to Jesus and he has taken me. "Is it so?" said he. "Then has a new flower blossomed in the kingdom this day." This is very sweet and beautiful and it shows that Dr. Beecher had a

tender heart under his Calvinistic theology.
" If she could have been let alone," says her
son, " and taught to ' look up and not down, for-
ward and not back, out and not in,' this religious
experience might have gone on as sweetly and
naturally as the opening of a flower in the
gentle rays of the sun. But unfortunately this
was not possible at a time when self-examination
was carried to an extreme that was calculated to
drive a nervous and sensitive child well-nigh
distracted. First, even her sister Catharine was
afraid that there might be something wrong in
the case of a lamb that had come into the fold
without being first chased all over the lot by the
shepherd: great stress being laid on what was
called being under conviction. Then also the
pastor of the First Church in Hartford, a bosom
friend of Dr. Beecher, looked with melancholy
and suspicious eyes on this unusual and doubtful
path to heaven."

Briefly stated, these two spiritual guides put
Harriet through a process which brought her to
a sense of sin that must have filled their hearts
with joy. She reached the stage when she wrote
to her brother Edward: " My whole life is one
continued struggle; I do nothing right. I am

beset behind and before, and my sins take away all my happiness."

Unfortunately for her, it was at this stage of Harriet's religious experience that Dr. Beecher was called to Boston to stem the rising tide of Unitarianism, with its easy notions about conviction of sin and other cardinal elements of a true faith. To be thrown into the fervors of a crusade was just the experience which Harriet's heated brain did not need. Her life at this period was divided between Hartford and Boston, but her heart went with Dr. Beecher to his great enterprise in Boston, or, as Mrs. Fields says, " This period in Boston was the time when Harriet felt she drew nearer to her father than at any other period of her life."

It will not be necessary to go farther into this controversy than to show what a cauldron it was for the family of Dr. Beecher. In his autobiography, Dr. Beecher says, " From the time Unitarianism began to show itself in this country, it was as fire in my bones." After his call to Boston, he writes again, " My mind had been heating, heating, heating. Now I had a chance to strike." The situation that confronted him in Boston rather inflamed than subdued his spirit. Let Mrs. Stowe tell the story

herself. " Calvinism or orthodoxy," she says,
" was the despised and persecuted form of faith.
It was the dethroned royal family wandering like
a permitted mendicant in the city where it once
held high court, and Unitarianism reigned in its
stead. All the literary men of Massachusetts
were Unitarians. All the trustees and profes-
sors of Harvard College were Unitarians. All
the élite of wealth and fashion crowded Unitarian churches. The judges on the bench were
Unitarian, giving decisions by which the peculiar features of church organization, so carefully
ordained by the Pilgrim Fathers, had been nulli-
fied. The dominant majority entered at once
into possession of churches and church property,
leaving the orthodox minority to go out into
schoolhouses and town halls, and build their
churches as best they could."

We can hardly suppose that Harriet had read
the decision of the court, or that she deemed it
necessary; she knew it was wrong by instinct,
and the iron entered her soul. The facts appear
to have been as follows: The old parishes in New
England included a given territory like a school
district or a voting precinct. Members of a
given parish, if they were communicants, formed
themselves into a " church " which was the

church of that parish. The court decided that this church always remained the church of that parish. Members might withdraw, but they withdrew as individuals. They could not withdraw the church, not even if they constituted a majority.

The correctness of this decision does not concern us here; it is enough that Dr. Beecher thought it wrong and that Harriet thought it wrong. "The effect of all this," she says, "upon my father's mind was to keep him at a white heat of enthusiasm. His family prayers at this period, departing from the customary forms of unexcited hours, became often upheavings of passionate emotion, such as I shall never forget. 'Come, Lord Jesus,' he would say, 'here where the bones of the fathers rest, here where the crown has been torn from thy brow, come and recall thy wandering children. Behold thy flock scattered upon the mountain — these sheep, what have they done! Gather them, gather them, O good shepherd, for their feet stumble upon the dark mountains.'"

The fierce heat of this period was too much for a tender plant like Harriet. For her state of mind, even Catharine thought the Boston home life was not entirely suitable. It would be better for her in Hartford. "Harriet will have young society here which she cannot have at home, and I think cheerful and amusing friends will do much for her." Catharine had received a letter from Harriet which, she says, "made me feel uneasy," as well it might. Harriet had written her sister: "I don't know as I am fit for anything, and I have thought that I could wish to die young and let the remembrance of me and my faults perish in the grave. . . . Sometimes I could not sleep, and have groaned and cried till midnight, while in the daytime I tried to appear cheerful, and succeeded so well that papa reproved me for laughing so much." Life was too serious to permit even an affectation of gaiety. "The atmosphere of that period," says Mrs. Field, "and the terrible arguments of her father and of her sister Catharine were sometimes more than she could endure." Her brother Edward was helpful and comforting. She thanks him for helping her solve some of her problems, but the situation was critical: "I feared that if you left me thus I might return to the same dark, desolate state in which I had been all summer. I felt that my immortal interest, my happiness for both worlds, was depending on the turn my feelings might take."

Dr. Beecher was too much absorbed with his mission to observe what was going on in his own family, unless there chanced to be an unexpected outburst of gaiety. " Every leisure hour was beset by people who came with earnest intention to express to him those various phases of weary, restless wandering desire proper to an earnest people whose traditional faith has been broken up. . . . Inquirers were constantly coming with every imaginable theological problem. . . . he was to be seen all day talking with whoever would talk. . . . till an hour or two before the time (of service), when he would rush up to his study; . . . just as the last stroke of the bell was dying away, he would emerge from the study with his coat very much awry, come down stairs like a hurricane, stand impatiently protesting while female hands that ever lay in wait adjusted his cravat and settled his collar. . . . and hooking wife or daughter like a satchel on his arm, away he would start on such a race through the streets as left neither brain nor breath till the church was gained." Such, very much abbreviated, is Mrs. Stowe's portrait of her father at this period. It is a good example of her power of delineation; but what a life was this for a half distracted girl like Harriet! Much better for her would have been the old serene, peaceful, quiet life of Litchfield.

She had several kinds of religious trouble. It troubled her that in the book of Job, God should seem " to have stripped a dependent creature of all that renders life desirable, and then to have answered his complaints from the whirlwind, and, instead of showing mercy and pity, to have overwhelmed him with a display of his power and justice." It troubled her that when she allowed herself to take a milder view of deity, " I feel," she says, " less fear of God and, in view of sin, I feel only a sensation of grief." This was an alarming decline. It troubled her again that she loved literature, whereas she ought only to care for religion. She writes to Edward: " You speak of your predilections for literature being a snare to you. I have found it so myself." Evidently, as she has before said, she was beset behind and before. What was perhaps worst of all, the heavens seemed closed to her. Calvinism was pure agnosticism; and she had been educated a Calvinist. There was no ' imminent God,' in all and through all, for Calvinism; that came in with Transcendentalism, a form of thought which

never seems to have touched Mrs. Stowe. She
seems always to have felt, as at this period she
writes Edward, that " still, after all, God is a
being afar off." Nevertheless, there was Christ,
but Christ at this period was also afar off: " I
feel that I love God,— that is that I love Christ,
— that I find happiness in it, and yet it is not
that kind of comfort which would arise from free
communication of my wants and sorrows to a
friend. I sometimes wish that the Savior were
visibly present in this world, that I might go to
him for a solution of some of my difficulties."

It will be seen from this passage that Harriet's
storm-tossed soul was settling down upon Christ
as the nearest approach to God one could gain
in the darkness, and with this she taught herself
to be content. " So, after four years of struggling and suffering," writes her son, " she returns to the place where she started from as a
child of thirteen. It has been like watching a
ship with straining masts and storm-beaten sails,
buffeted by the waves, making for the harbor,
and coming at last to quiet anchorage." One
cannot help reflecting how different would have
been her experience in the household of Dr.
Channing; but Dr. Beecher would sooner have
trusted her in a den of wolves.

Harriet was seventeen years old when, mentally, she reached her quiet anchorage but, physically as might be expected, it was with a constitution undermined and with health broken. " She had not grown to be a strong woman," says Mrs. Fields; " the apparently healthy and hearty child had been suffered to think and feel, to study and starve (as we say), starve for relaxation, until she became a woman of much suffering and many inadequacies of physical life." A year or two later Harriet herself writes, " This inner world of mine has become worn out and untenable," and again, " About half my time I am scarcely alive. . . . I have everything but good health. . . . Thought, intense emotional thought, has been my disease."

At the end of six restless and stormy years, in 1832, Dr. Beecher resigned his Boston pastorate to accept the presidency of Lane Theological Seminary at Cincinnati, Ohio, Catharine and Harriet accompanying the family with the purpose of establishing a high grade school for young women. The plan was successfully carried out, and the " Western Female Institute " marked a new stage in education west of the Alleghenies. One of Harriet's early achievements at Cincinnati was the publication of a text-book in geography, her first attempt at authorship. She made her entry into the field of imaginative literature by gaining a prize of $50 for a story printed in *The Western Magazine*.

Her connection with the "Western Female Institute" was brief, and the prosecution of a literary career was postponed, by her marriage in 1836, with Prof. Calvin E. Stowe; or, as she announces this momentous event: "about half an hour more and your old friend, schoolmate, sister, etc., will cease to be Hattie Beecher and change to nobody knows who."

The married life of Mrs. Stowe covered a period of fifty years and was a conspicuously happy one. Prof. Stowe, who seemed so much like a myth to the general public, was a man of great learning and keen intelligence, unimaginative as he says himself, but richly endowed with "a certain broad humor and drollery." His son tells us that he was "an inimitable mimic and story-teller. No small proportion of Mrs. Stowe's success as a literary woman is to be attributed to him." The Sam Lawson stories are said to be a little more his than hers, being "told as they came from Mr. Stowe's lips with little or no alteration." For her scholarly husband, Mrs.

Stowe had the highest appreciation and the prettiest way of expressing it: " If you were not already my dearly loved husband," she writes him, " I should certainly fall in love with you." Prof. Stowe could also write a love-letter: " There is no woman like you in this wide world. Who else has so much talent with so little self-conceit; so much reputation with so little affectation; so much literature with so little nonsense; so much enterprise with so little extravagance; so much tongue with so little scold; so much sweetness with so little softness; so much of so many things and so little of so many other things." If a man's wife is to have her biography written, he will not be sorry that he has sent her some effusive love-letters.

Fourteen years of Mrs. Stowe's beautiful married life were spent in Cincinnati, with many vicissitudes of ill-health, some poverty, and the birth of six children, three sons and three daughters. One can get some idea both of the happiness and the hardship of that life from her letters. In 1843, seven years after marriage, she writes, " Our straits for money this year are unparalleled even in our annals. Even our bright and cheery neighbor Allen begins to look blue, and says $600 is the very most we can hope to collect of our salary, once $1,200." Again she writes, "I am already half sick from confinement to the house and overwork. If I should sew every day for a month to come I should not be able to accomplish half of what is to be done." There were trials enough during this period, but her severest affliction came in its last year, in the loss of an infant son by cholera. That was in 1849, when Cincinnati was devastated; when during the months of June, July and August more than nine thousand persons died of cholera within three miles of her house, and among them she says, "My Charley, my beautiful, loving, gladsome baby, so loving, so sweet, so full of life and hope and strength."

In these years, Mrs. Stowe's life was too full of domestic care to permit many excursions into the field of literature. In 1842, a collection of sketches was published by the Harpers under the title of the "Mayflower." Occasionally she contributed a bright little story to a monthly or an annual. An amusing account is given of the writing of one of these stories, by a lady who volunteered to serve as amanuensis while Mrs. Stowe dictated, and at the same time supervised a new girl in the kitchen: "You may now write," said Mrs. Stowe, 'Her lover wept with her, nor dared he again touch the point so sacredly guarded — (Mina, roll that crust a little thinner). He spoke in soothing tones.— (Mina, poke the coals).' "

These literary efforts, produced under difficulties, inspired Prof. Stowe with great confidence in her genius. He wrote her in 1842, " My dear, you must be a literary woman. It is so written in the book of fate." Again he writes, " God has written it in his book that you must be a literary woman, and who are we that we should contend against God! You must therefore make all your calculations to spend the rest of your life with your pen." Nevertheless the next eight years pass as the last six have passed without apparently bringing the dream of a literary career nearer fulfilment. With a few strokes of the pen, Mrs. Stowe draws a picture of her life at this period: " I was married when I was twenty-five years old to a man rich in Greek and Hebrew and, alas, rich in nothing else. . . . During long years of struggling with poverty and sickness, and a hot, debilitating climate, my children grew up around me. The nursery and the kitchen were my principal fields of labor. Some of my friends, pitying my trials, copied and sent a number of little sketches from my pen to certain liberally paying annuals, with my name. With the first money that I earned in this way I bought a feather bed! for as I had married into poverty and without a dowry, and as my husband had only a large library of books and a good deal of learning, the bed and pillows were thought the most profitable investment. After this I thought that I had discovered the philosopher's stone. So when a new carpet or mattress was going to be needed, or when at the close of the year it began to be evident that my family accounts, like poor Dora's, 'wouldn't add up,' then I used to say to my faithful friend and factotum Anna, who shared all my joys and sorrows, ' Now, if you will keep the babies and attend to things in the house for a day, I'll write a piece and then we'll be out of the scrape.' So I became an author,— very modest I do assure you."

The hardships and privations of Mrs. Stowe's residence in Cincinnati were more than compensated to her by the opportunity it afforded for intimate acquaintance with the negro character and personal observation of the institution of slavery. Only the breadth of the Ohio river separated her from Kentucky, a slave State. While yet a teacher in the Female Institute, she spent a vacation upon a Kentucky estate, afterward graphically described in 'Uncle Tom's Cabin' as Col. Shelby's plantation. A companion upon this visit said, "Harriet did not seem to notice anything in particular that happened. · · · Afterwards, in reading 'Uncle Tom,' I recognized scene after scene of that visit portrayed with the most minute fidelity." A dozen years before there were any similar demonstrations in Boston, she witnessed in 1838, pro-slavery riots in Cincinnati when Birney's Abolition press was wrecked and when Henry Ward Beecher, then a young Cincinnati editor, went armed to and from his office. She had had in her service a slave girl whose master was searching the city for her, and whose rescue had been effected by Prof. Stowe and Henry Ward Beecher who, "both armed, drove the fugitive, in a covered wagon, by night, by unfrequented roads, twelve miles back into the country, and left her in safety." This incident was the basis of "the fugitive's escape from Tom Loker and Marks in 'Uncle Tom's Cabin.'"

Lane Theological Seminary, in which Prof. Stowe held a chair, had, it is said, "become a hot-bed of abolition." Partly for protection, a colony of negroes had settled about the seminary, and these families, says Mrs. Stowe, " be- came my favorite resort in cases of emergency. If anyone wishes to have a black face look hand- some, let them be left as I have been, in feeble health, in oppressive hot weather, with a sick baby in arms, and two other ones in the nursery, and not a servant in the whole house to do a turn." " Time would fail me," writes Mrs. Stowe, " to tell you all that I learned incidental- ly of the slave system in the history of various slaves who came into my family, and of the un- derground railroad which, I may say, ran through our house."

A New England education alone would not have given Mrs. Stowe the material to write the story of " Uncle Tom." A youth passed on a Southern plantation would have made her cal- lous and indifferent, as it did so many tender- hearted women. A New England woman of genius, educated in New England traditions, was providentially transferred to the heated border line between freedom and slavery and, during eighteen years, made to hear a thousand authen- tic incidents of the patriarchal system from the victims themselves. Then " Uncle Tom's Cabin " could be written. Perhaps one other element of preparation ought to be mentioned since Mrs.

Stowe laid stress upon it herself. The woman who should write " Uncle Tom's Cabin " needed to be a mother who had known what it is to have a child snatched from her arms irrevocably and without a moment's notice. It was at her baby's " dying bed and at his grave that I learned," she says, " what a poor slave mother may feel when her child is torn away from her. In those depths of sorrow which seemed to me immeasurable, it was my only prayer to God that such anguish might not be suffered in vain. . . . I allude to this because I have often felt that much that is in that book ('Uncle Tom') had its roots in the awful scenes and bitter sorrows of that summer."

In 1850, this western life, with its mixture of sweet and bitter waters, came to an end. The climate of Cincinnati was unfavorable to the health of both Mr. and Mrs. Stowe, and Mr. Stowe accepted a professorship in Bowdoin College, at the small salary of $1,000 a year, declining at the same time an offer from New York city of $2,300. Why he accepted the smaller salary is not said. Certainly it assured him his old felicity, his Master's blessing upon the poor. The situation, however, was better than it seems, as Mrs. Stowe had written enough to have confidence in her pen, and she purposed to make the family income at least $1,700 by her writings. She accomplished much more than that as we shall presently see.

From the car window, as one passes through Brunswick, Maine, he can see the house in which Mrs. Stowe passed the three following very happy years, in which her seventh child was born, a son who lived to be her biographer, and in which she wrote "Uncle Tom's Cabin." It will be remembered that the year 1850 was made memorable by the enactment of the Fugitive Slave Law. How the attempted execution of this law affected Mrs. Stowe can be anticipated. "To me," she says, "it is incredible, amazing, mournful. I feel as if I should be willing to sink with it, were all this sin and misery to sink in the sea. . . . I sobbed aloud in one pew and Mrs. Judge Reeves in another."

In this mood, Mrs. Stowe received a letter from Mrs. Edward Beecher saying, "Hattie, if I could use a pen as you can, I would write something to make this nation feel what an accursed thing slavery is." Her children remember that at the reading of this letter, Mrs. Stowe rose from her chair, crushing the letter in her hand, and said, "I will write something,— I

will if I live." The fulfilment of this vow was
" Uncle Tom's Cabin."

This story was begun in *The National Era,* on
June 5, 1851; it was announced to run through
three months and it occupied ten. " I could not
control the story," said Mrs. Stowe; " it wrote
itself." Again, she said, " I the author of
' Uncle Tom's Cabin!' No, indeed. The Lord
himself wrote it, and I was but the humblest instrument in his hand." It has been said that
" ' Uncle Tom's Cabin ' made the crack of the
slave-driver's whip and the cries of the tortured
blacks ring in every household in the land, till
human hearts could bear it no longer," and that
it " made the enforcement of the Fugitive Slave
Law an impossibility."

It is possible to discuss the question whether
" Uncle Tom's Cabin " is a work of art, just as it
is possible to discuss whether the Sermon on the
Mount is a work of art, but not whether the
story was effective, not whether it hit the mark
and accomplished its purpose. Mrs. Stowe's
story is not so much one story as a dozen; in the
discriminating language of her son, it is " a
series of pictures," and who will deny that the
scenes are skilfully portrayed!

Mrs. Stowe did not know that she had made

her fortune; she had not written for money; nevertheless when the story was republished in a volume, her ten per cent. of the profits brought her $10,000 in four months. It went to its third edition in ten days, and one hundred and twenty editions, or more than 300,000 copies were sold in this country within one year. This astounding popularity was exceeded in Great Britain. Not being protected by copyright, eighteen publishing houses issued editions varying from 6d to 15s a copy, and in twelve months, more than a million and a half of copies had been sold in the British dominions. The book was also translated and published in nineteen European languages. It was dramatized and brought out in New York in 1852, and, a year later it was running still. "Everybody goes," it was said, "night after night and nothing can stop it." In London, in 1852, it was the attraction at two theatres.

What the public thought of the story is evident, nor did competent judges dissent. Longfellow said: "It is one of the greatest triumphs recorded in literary history, to say nothing of the higher triumph of its moral effect." George Sand said: "Mrs. Stowe is all instinct; it is the very reason that she appears to some to have no talent. . . . I cannot say that she has talent as one understands it in the world of letters, but she has genius as humanity feels the need of it,— the genius of goodness, not that of the man of letters, but of the saint. . . . In matters of art, there is but one rule, to paint and to move." I give but a paragraph of a paper which Senator Sumner called " a most remarkable tribute, such as was hardly ever offered by such a genius to any living mortal."

Apologists for the slave system have declared that " Uncle Tom's Cabin " is a libel upon the system. One must do that before he can begin his apology; but the remarkable fact is that not even in the South was the libel detected at the first. That was an after-thought. Whittier knew a lady who read the story " to some twenty young ladies, daughters of slave-holders, near New Orleans and amid the scenes described in it, and they with one accord pronounced it true." It was not till the sale of the book had run to over 100,000 copies that a reaction set in and then, strange to say, the note of warning was sounded by that infallible authority upon American affairs, the London Times.

In 1852, the year following the publication of " Uncle Tom " Prof. Stowe accepted a chair in the Theological Seminary at Andover, and that village became the home of the family during the ten following happy years. In 1853, Mr. and Mrs. Stowe went to England upon the invitation of Anti-slavery friends who guaranteed and considerably overpaid the expenses of the trip. " Should Mrs. Stowe conclude to visit Europe," wrote Senator Sumner, " she will have a triumph." The prediction was fulfilled. At Liverpool she is met by friends and breakfasted with a little company of thirty or forty people; at Glasgow, she drinks tea with two thousand; at Edinburgh there was " another great tea party," and she was presented with a " national penny offering consisting of a thousand golden sovereigns on a magnificent silver salver." She had the Highlands yet to see as the guest of the Duke of Argyll, not to mention London and Paris. After five months, she sailed from Liverpool on her return, and is it any wonder that she wrote, " Almost sadly as a child might leave its home, I left the shores of kind, strong Old England, the mother of us all ! "

In 1856, Mrs. Stowe visited Europe a second time for the purpose of securing an English copyright upon " Dred," having learned something of business by her experience with " Uncle

Tom." It will be interesting to know that in England "Dred" was considered the better story, that 100,000 copies of it were sold there in four weeks, and that her English publisher issued it in editions of 125,000 copies each. "After that," writes Mrs. Stowe, "who cares what the critics say?"

She was abroad nearly a year, visiting France, Switzerland, and Italy, and returned in June, 1857, to experience another sad bereavement. Her son Henry was a Freshman in Dartmouth college and, while bathing in the Connecticut river, he was drowned. This was a severe trial to Mrs. Stowe and the more so because, whatever her religion may have done for her, the theology in which she had been educated gave no comfort to her soul. "Distressing doubts as to Henry's spiritual state were rudely thrust upon my soul." These doubts she was able to master at least temporarily, by assuming that they were temptations of the devil, but three years later in Florence, on a third voyage to Europe, she wrote her husband, in reply to his allusions to Henry, "Since I have been in Florence, I have been distressed by inexpressible yearnings for him,—such sighings and outreachings, with a sense of utter darkness and separation, not only from him

but from all spiritual communion with my God."
It will be interesting to know that relief was
brought her in this painful crisis, by the ministrations of spiritualism.

Mrs. Stowe returned in 1860 from her third
visit to Europe to find the country hovering upon
the verge of Civil War. The war brought her
another sore bereavement. At the battle of Get-
tysburg, her son, Capt. Frederick Stowe, was
struck by the fragment of a shell and, though
the wound healed, he never really recovered.
His end was sufficiently tragic. With the hope
of improving his health by a long sea voyage,
he sailed from New York for San Francisco by
way of Cape Horn. That he reached San Francisco in safety, writes his brother, " is known:
but that is all. No word from him or concerning
him has ever reached the loving hearts that have
waited so anxiously for it, and of his ultimate
fate nothing is known." Whatever may have
been the " spiritual state " of this son, Mrs.
Stowe had now somewhat modernized her theology and could say, " An endless infliction for
past sins was once the doctrine that we now generally reject. . . . Of one thing I am sure,
— probation does not end with this life." To

stamp out that very heresy had been no small part of Dr. Beecher's mission in Boston.

In 1863, Prof. Stowe having resigned his chair in Andover, Mrs. Stowe removed with her family to Hartford where for the remaining thirty-three years of her life, she made her summer home. The winter of 1866, she spent with her husband in Florida and, the year following, she bought in that semi-tropical state an orange orchard, the fruit of which the year previous had " brought $2,000 as sold at the wharf." Here for sixteen winters Mr. and Mrs. Stowe made their home, until her " poor rabbi," as she affectionately calls him, became too feeble to bear the long journey from Hartford. There she built a small Episcopal church and she invites her brother Charles to become an Episcopalian and come and be her minister.

Her son says that " Mrs. Stowe had some years before this joined the Episcopal church for the purpose of attending the same communion as her daughters." That she desired to attend the same communion as her daughters does not seem a sufficient reason for leaving the communion of her husband. Certainly, she had other reasons. From her fourth year, she had known the service and, as read by her grandmother at that time, its prayers "had a different effect upon me," she says, "from any other prayers I heard in early life." Moreover, she had a mission to the negro race and believed that the Episcopal service is specially adapted to their needs: "If my tasks and feelings did not incline me toward the Church," she writes her brother, "I should still choose it as the best system for training immature minds such as those of our negroes. The system was composed with reference to the wants of the laboring class of England, at a time when they were as ignorant as our negroes are now."

The picture of her southern life which she gives in a letter to George Eliot, is very attractive, her husband "sitting on the veranda reading all day," but during these years, Mrs. Stowe must have spent much of her own time at a writing-table since, for the ten years after 1867, when the Florida life began, she published a volume, sometimes two volumes, a year. In 1872, she was tempted by the Boston Lecture Bureau to give readings from her own works in the principal cities of New England, and the following year, the course was repeated in the cities of the West. Her audiences were to her amazing. "And how they do laugh! We get into regular gales," she writes her lonely husband at home.

Her seventieth birthday was celebrated at a gathering of two hundred of the leading literary men and women of the land, at the residence of Ex-Governor Claflin in Newton. There were poems by Whittier, Dr. Holmes, J. T. Trowbridge, Mrs. Whitney, Elizabeth Stuart Phelps, Mrs. Fields, and others, many excellent speeches, and finally a speech by the little woman herself. This garden party, says her son, was the last public appearance of Mrs. Stowe.

Her " rabbi " left her a widow in 1886, dying at the age of 84. Mrs. Stowe survived him ten years, dying in 1896, at the age of 85, leaving behind her a name loved and honored upon two continents.

VII
LOUISA MAY ALCOTT

LOUISA MAY ALCOTT

Miss Alcott has been called, perhaps truly, the most popular story-teller for children, in her generation. Like those elect souls whom the apostle saw arrayed in white robes, she came up through great tribulation, paying dearly in labor and privation for her successes, but one must pronounce her life happy and fortunate, since she lived to enjoy her fame and fortune twenty years, to witness the sale of a million volumes of her writings, to receive more than two hundred thousand dollars from her publishers, and thereby to accomplish the great purpose upon which as a girl she had set her heart, which was, to see her father and mother comfortable in their declining years.

Successful as Miss Alcott was as a writer, she was greater as a woman, and the story of her life is as interesting,— as full of tragedy and comedy,— as the careers of her heroes and heroines. In fact, we have reason to believe that the adventures of her characters are often not so much invented, as remembered, the pranks and frolics of her boys and girls being episodes from her own youthful experience. In the preface to " Little Women," the most charming of her books, she tells us herself that the most improbable incidents are the least imaginary. The happy girlhood which she portrays was her own, in spite of forbidding conditions. The struggle in which her cheerful nature extorted happiness from unwilling fortune, gives a dramatic interest to her youthful experiences, as her literary disappointments and successes do to the years of her maturity.

Miss Alcott inherited a name which her father's genius had made known on both sides of the sea, before her own made it famous in a hundred thousand households. Alcott is a derivative from Alcocke, the name by which Mr. Alcott himself was known in his boyhood. John Alcocke, born in New Haven, Ct., married Mary, daughter of Rev. Abraham Pierson, first president of Yale College. He was a man of considerable fortune and left 1,200 acres of land to his six children, one of whom was Capt. John Alcocke, a man of some distinction in the colonial service. Joseph Chatfield Alcocke, son of Capt. John, married Anna, sister of Rev. Tillotson Bronson, D.D. Of this marriage, Amos

LOUISA MAY ALCOTT

Bronson Alcott, father of Louisa, was born, Nov. 29, 1799. The fortunes of Joseph Chatfield Alcocke were those of other small farmers of the period, but Mrs. Alcocke could not forget that she was the sister of a college graduate, and it was worth something to her son to know that he was descended from the president of a college. The mother and son early settled it that the boy should be a scholar, and the father loyally furthered their ambitions, borrowing of his acquaintances such books as he discovered and bringing them home for the delectation of his studious son. At the age of thirteen, Bronson became a pupil in a private school kept by his uncle, Dr. Bronson, and at eighteen, he set out for Virginia with the secret purpose of teaching if opportunity offered, at the same time taking along a peddler's trunk out of which to turn an honest penny and pay the expenses of his journey. Circumstances did not favor his becoming a Virginia teacher, but between his eighteenth and twenty-third years, he made several expeditions into the Southern States as a Yankee peddler, with rather negative financial results, but with much enlargement of his information and improvement of his rustic manners. Mr. Alcott was rather distinguished for his high-bred manners and, on a visit to England, there is an amusing incident of his having been mistaken for some member of the titled aristocracy.

At the age of twenty-five, Mr. Alcott began his career as a teacher in an Episcopal Academy at Cheshire, Ct. His family were Episcopalians, and he had been confirmed at sixteen. Since the age of eighteen when he started for Virginia as a candidate for a school, he had been theorizing upon the art of teaching and had thought out many of the principles of what, a century later, began to be called the " New Education." He undertook, perhaps too rapidly, to apply his theories in the conduct of the Cheshire Academy. His experiments occasioned a vast amount of controversy, in which Connecticut conservatism gained a victory, and Mr. Alcott retired from the school at the end of two years' service. His results however had been sufficient to convince him of the soundness of his principles, and to launch him upon the troubled career of educational reform.

Among a few intelligent friends and sympathizers who rallied to Mr. Alcott's side in this controversy, was Rev. Samuel J. May, a Unitarian minister then of Brooklyn, Ct., at whose house, in 1827, Mr. Alcott met Mr. May's sister

Abbie, who shared fully her brother's enthusiasm
for the new education and its persecuted apostle.
Miss May began her relations with Mr. Alcott
as his admirer and champion, a dangerous part
for an enthusiastic young lady to play, as the
sequel proved when, three years later, she became Mrs. Alcott.

Mrs. Alcott was the daughter of a Boston
merchant, Col. Joseph May, and his wife, Dorothy Sewall, daughter of Samuel Sewall and his
wife, Elizabeth Quincy, sister of Dorothy
Quincy, wife of John Hancock. By the marriage of Joseph May and Dorothy Sewall, two
very distinguished lines of ancestry had been
united. Under her father's roof, Mrs. Alcott
had enjoyed every comfort and the best of social advantages. She was tall, had a fine phy-
sique, good intellect, warm affections, and generous sympathies, but it would have astonished
her to have been told that she was bringing to
the marriage altar more than she received; and
however much it may have cost her to be the
wife of an unworldly idealist, it was precisely
his unworldly idealism that first won her admiration and then gained her heart.

Life may have been harder for Mrs. Alcott
than she anticipated, but she knew very well

that she was abjuring riches.   Two years before her marriage, her brother had written her: "Mr. Alcott's mind and heart are so much occupied with other things that poverty and riches do not seem to concern him much." She had known Mr. Alcott three years and had enjoyed ample opportunity to make this observation herself.   Indeed, two months after her marriage, she wrote her brother, "My husband is the perfect personification of modesty and moderation. I am not sure that we shall not blush into obscurity and contemplate into starvation." That she had not repented of her choice a year later, may be judged from a letter to her brother on the first anniversary of her marriage: "It has been an eventful year,— a year of trial, of happiness, of improvement.   I can wish no better fate to any sister of my sex than has attended me since my entrance into the conjugal state."

That Mr. Alcott, then in his young manhood, had qualities which, for a young lady of refinement and culture, would compensate for many privations is evident.   Whether he was one of the great men of his generation or not, there is no doubt he seemed so.   When, in 1837, Dr. Bartol came to Boston, Mr. Emerson asked him whom he knew in the city, and said: "There is but one man, Mr. Alcott." Dr. Bartol seems to have come to much the same opinion. He says: "Alcott belonged to the Christ class: his manners were the most gentle and gracious, under all fair or unfair provocation, I ever beheld; he had a rare inborn piety and a god-like incapacity in the purity of his eyes to behold iniquity."

These qualities were not visible to the public and have no commercial value, but that Mr. Alcott had them is confirmed by the beautiful domestic life of the Alcotts, by the unabated love and devotion of Mrs. Alcott to her husband in all trials, and the always high and always loyal appreciation with which Louisa speaks of her father, even when perhaps smiling at his innocent illusions. The character of Mr. Alcott is an important element in the life of Louisa because she was his daughter, and because, being unmarried, her life and fortunes were his, or those of the Alcott family. She had no individual existence.

Two years after the marriage of Mr. and Mrs. Alcott, Louisa, their second daughter was born in Germantown, Pa., where Mr. Alcott was in charge of a school belonging to the Society of Friends, or Quakers. The date was November 29, 1832, also Mr. Alcott's birthday, always observed as a double festival in the family. In 1834, Mr. Alcott opened his celebrated school in Masonic Temple in Boston, Mass., under the auspices of Dr. Channing and with the assured patronage of some of the most cultivated and influential families in the city. As assistants in this school, he had first Miss Sophia Peabody afterward Mrs. Hawthorne, her sister Miss Elizabeth Peabody, and finally Margaret Fuller.

The school opened prosperously and achieved remarkable success until, in 1837, the publication of Mr. Alcott's "Conversations on the Gospels " shocked the piety of Boston newspapers, whose persistent and virulent attacks frightened the public and caused the withdrawal of two-thirds of the pupils. Mr. Emerson came to Mr. Alcott's defence, saying: " He is making an experiment in which all the friends of education are interested," and asking, " whether it be wise or just to add to the anxieties of this enterprise a public clamor against some detached sentences of a book which, on the whole, is pervaded by original thought and sincere piety." In a private note, Mr. Emerson urged Mr. Alcott to give up his school, as the people of Boston were

not worthy of him. Mr. Alcott had spent more
than the income of the school in its equipment,
creating debts which Louisa afterward paid;
all his educational ideals were at stake, and he
could not accept defeat easily. However, in
1839, a colored girl was admitted to the school,
and all his pupils were withdrawn, except the
little negress and four whites, three of whom
were his own daughters. So ended the Temple
school. The event was very fateful for the Alcott family, but, much as it concerned Mrs.
Alcott, there can be no doubt she much preferred
that the school should end thus, than that Mr.
Alcott should yield to public clamor on either of
the issues which wrecked the enterprise.

Louisa was seven years old when this misfor-
tune occurred which shaped the rest of her life,
fixing the straitened circumstances in which she
was to pass her youth and preparing the burdens which ultimately were to be lifted by her
facile pen. Happily the little Alcotts, of whom
there were three, were too young to feel the per-
plexities that harassed their parents and their
early years could hardly have been passed more
pleasantly or profitably if they had been the
daughters of millionaires. The family lived
very comfortably amidst a fine circle of relatives

and friends in Boston, preached and practised a vegetarian gospel,— rice without sugar and graham meal without butter or molasses,— monotonous but wholesome, spent their summers with friends at Scituate and, in town or country, partly owing to the principles of the new education, partly to the preoccupation of the parents, the children of the family were left in large measure to the teaching of nature and their own experience.

Very abundant moral instruction there was in this apostolic family, both by example and precept, but the young disciples were expected to make their own application of the principles. The result, in the case of Louisa, was to develop a girl of very enterprising and adventurous character, who might have been mistaken for a boy from her sun-burned face, vigorous health, and abounding animal spirits. It was her pride to drive her hoop around the Common before breakfast and she tells us that she admitted to her social circle no girl who could not climb a tree and no boy whom she had not beaten in a race. Her autobiography of this period, she has given us, very thinly disguised, in "Poppy's Pranks."

Meanwhile, her mental faculties were not

neglected. Mr. Alcott began the education of his children, in a kindergarten way, almost in their infancy, and before his Boston school closed, Louisa had two or three years in it as a pupil. What his method of education could do with a child of eight years is shown by a poem written by Louisa at that age. The family were then living in Concord, in the house which, in "Little Women," is celebrated as "Meg's first home." One early Spring day, Louisa found in the garden a robin, chilled and famished, and wrote these lines:

> "Welcome, welcome, little stranger,
> Fear no harm, and fear no danger;
> We are glad to see you here,
> For you sing, Sweet Spring is near.
>
> Now the white snow melts away;
> Now the flowers blossom gay:
> Come, dear bird, and build your nest,
> For we love our robin best."

It will be remembered that this literary faculty, unusual at the age of eight, had been attained by a girl in the physical condition of an athlete, who could climb a tree like a squirrel.

Readers of "Little Women" will remember what a child's paradise "Meg's first home" was, with its garden full of fruit-trees and shade, and its old empty barn which the children alternately turned into a drawing-room for company, a gymnasium for romps, and a theatre for dramatic performances. " There," says Louisa, " we dramatized the fairy tales in great style," Jack the Giant-killer and Cinderella being favorites, the passion for the stage which came near making Louisa an actress, as also her sister Anna, getting early development.

The fun and frolic of these days were the more enjoyed because they alternated with regular duties, with lessons in housework with the mother and language lessons with the father, for which he now had abundant leisure. As he had no other pupils, he could try all his educational experiments in his own family. Among other exercises, the children were required to keep a journal, to write in it regularly, and to submit it to the examination and criticism of the parents. Facility in writing thus became an early acquisition. It was furthered by a pretty habit which Mrs. Alcott had of keeping up a little correspondence with her children, writing little notes to them when she had anything to say in the way of reproof, correction, or instruction, receiving their confessions, repentance, and good resolutions by the next mail.

Some of these maternal letters are very tender and beautiful. One to Louisa at the age of eleven, enclosed a picture of a frail mother cared for by a faithful daughter, and says, " I have always liked it very much, for I imagined that you might be just such an industrious daughter and I such a feeble and loving mother, looking to your labor for my daily bread." There was prophecy in this and there was more prophecy in the lines with which Louisa replied:

" I hope that soon, dear mother,
    You and I may be
In the quiet room my fancy
    Has so often made for thee,—

The pleasant, sunny chamber,
    The cushioned easy-chair,
The book laid for your reading,
    The vase of flowers fair;

The desk beside the window
    When the sun shines warm and bright,
And there in ease and quiet,
    The promised book you write.

While I sit close beside you,
    Content at last to see
That you can rest, dear mother,
    And I can cherish thee."

The versification is still juvenile, but there is no fault in the sentiment, and Miss Alcott, in a later note, says, " The dream came true, and for the last ten years of her life, Marmee sat in peace with every wish granted."

Evidently Louisa had begun to feel the pinch of the family circumstances. The income was of the slenderest. Sometimes Mr. Alcott gave a lecture or " conversation " and received a few dollars; sometimes he did a day's farm work for a neighbor; now and then Mr. Emerson called and clandestinely left a bank note, and many valuable packages came out from relatives in Boston; but frugal housekeeping was the chief asset of the family. Discouraging as the outlook was, some bitter experience might have been escaped if the Alcotts had remained in Concord, pursuing their unambitious career. It was, however, the era of social experiments in New England. The famous Brook Farm community was then in the third year of its existence, and it was impossible that Mr. Alcott should not sympathize with this effort to ease the burden of life, and wish to try his own experiment. Therefore, in 1843, being joined by several English socialists, one of whom financed the undertaking, Mr. Alcott started a small community on a worn-out not to say abandoned farm, which was hopefully christened " Fruitlands."

Visiting the community five or six weeks after its inception, Mr. Emerson wrote: " The sun and the evening sky do not look calmer than Alcott and his family at Fruitlands. They seem to have arrived at the fact,— to have got rid of the show, and so to be serene. They look well in July; we will see them in December." An inhospitable December came upon the promising experiment, as it generally has upon all similar enterprises. Under the title Transcendental Wild Oats, in " Silver Pitchers," Miss Alcott gives a lively account of the varying humors of this disastrous adventure.

Whatever disappointments and privations the enterprise had in store for their parents, the situation, with its little daily bustle, its limitless range of fields and woods, its flower hunting and berry picking, was full of interest and charm for four healthy children all under the age of twelve years. The fateful December, to which Mr. Emerson postponed his judgment, had not come before the elders were debating a dissolution of the community. " Father asked us if we saw any reason for us to separate," writes Louisa in her journal. " Mother wanted to, she is so tired. I like it." Of course she did; but "not the school part," she adds, "nor Mr. L.", who was one of her teachers. The inevitable lessons interfered with her proper business.

"Fruitlands" continued for three years with declining fortunes, its lack of promise being perhaps a benefit to the family in saving for other purposes a small legacy which Mrs. Alcott received from her father's estate. With this and a loan of $500 from Mr. Emerson, she bought "The Hillside" in Concord, an estate which, after the Alcotts, was occupied by Mr. Hawthorne. Thither Mrs. Alcott removed with her family in 1846, and the two years that followed is the period which Louisa looked back upon as the happiest of her life, "for we had," she says, "charming playmates in the little Emersons, Channings, Hawthornes, and Goodwins, with the illustrious parents and their friends to enjoy our pranks and share our excursions." Here the happy girlish life was passed which is so charmingly depicted in "Little Women," and here at the age of sixteen, Louisa wrote, for the entertainment of the little Alcotts and Emersons, a series of pretty fairy tales, still to be read in the second volume of Lulu's Library.

Much as there was to enjoy in these surroundings, the problem of subsistence had not been solved and, with the growth of her daughters toward womanhood, it became more difficult for Mrs. Alcott. The world had, apparently, no use for Mr. Alcott; there were six persons to be fed and clothed, and no bread-winner in the family. The story is that one day, a friend found her in tears and demanded an explanation. " Abby Alcott, what does this mean? " asked the visitor, and when Mrs. Alcott had made her confessions, her friend said, " Come to Boston and I will find you employment."

Accepting the proposition, the family removed to Boston in 1848, and Mrs. Alcott became the agent of certain benevolent societies. Mr. Alcott taught private classes, or held " conversations "; the older daughters, Anna and Louisa, found employment; and we may think of the family as fairly comfortable during the seven or eight years of its life in Boston. " Our poor little home," says Miss Alcott, " had much love and happiness in it, and was a shelter for lost girls, abused wives, friendless children, and weak and wicked men. Father and mother had no money to give but they gave time, sympathy, help; and if blessings would make them rich, they would be millionaires." Fugitive slaves were among the homeless who found shelter, one of whom Mrs. Alcott concealed in an unused brick oven.

In Miss Alcott's journal of this period, we find the burden of existence weighing very heavily upon her, a state of mind apparently induced by her first expereince in teaching. "School is hard work," she says, "and I feel as though I should like to run away from it. But my children get on; so I travel up every day and do my best. I get very little time to write or think, for my working days have begun." Later, she seems to have seen the value of this experience. "At sixteen," she writes, "I began to teach twenty pupils and, for ten years, I learned to know and love children."

Amateur theatricals were still the recreation of the Alcott girls, as they had been almost from infancy, and the stage presented a fascinating alternative to the school-room. "Anna wants to be an actress and so do I," writes Louisa at seventeen. "We could make plenty of money perhaps, and it is a very gay life. Mother says we are too young and must wait. Anna acts splendidly. I like tragic plays and shall be a Siddons if I can. We get up harps, dresses, water-falls, and thunder, and have great fun."

Both of the sisters wrote many exciting dramas at this period, and one of Louisa's, " The Rival Prima Donnas," was accepted by the manager of the Boston Theatre, who " thought it would have a fine run " and sent the author a free pass to the theatre, which partly compensated for the non-appearance of the play. Some years later, a farce written by Louisa, " Nat Bachelor's Pleasure Trip, or the Trials of a Good-Natured Man," was produced at the Howard Athenæum, and was favorably received. Christie's experience as an actress, in Miss Alcott's novel entitled, " Work," is imaginary in its incidents, but autobiographical in its spirit.

All these experiments in dramatic literature, from Jack the Giant-Killer on, were training the future story-teller. Miss Alcott's first story to see the light was printed in a newspaper at the age of twenty, in 1852, though it had been written at sixteen. She received $5.00 for it, and the event is interesting as the beginning of her fortune. This little encouragement came at a period of considerable trial for the family. The following is from her journal of 1853 : " In January, I started a little school of about a dozen in our parlor. In May, my school closed and I went to L. as second girl. I needed the change, could do the wash, and was glad to earn my $2.00 a week." Notice that this is her summer vacation. " Home in October with $34.00 for my wages. After two days' rest, began school again with ten children." The family distributed themselves as follows: " Anna went to Syracuse to teach; father to the west to try his luck,— so poor, so hopeful, so serene. God be with him. Mother had several boarders. School for me, month after month. I earned a good deal by sewing in the evening when my day's work was done."

Mr. Alcott returned from the west, and the account of his adventures is very touching: " In February father came home. Paid his way, but no more. A dramatic scene when he arrived in the night. We were awakened by the bell. Mother flew down crying, My Husband. We rushed after and five white figures embraced the half-frozen wanderer who came in, hungry, tired, cold, and disappointed, but smiling bravely and as serene as ever. We fed and warmed and brooded over him, longing to ask if he had made any money; but no one did till little May said, after he had told us all the pleasant things, ' Well, did people pay you? ' Then with a queer look he opened his pocket book, and showed one dollar, saying with a smile, ' Only that. My overcoat was stolen, and I had to buy a shawl. Many promises were not kept, and traveling is costly ; but I have opened the way, and another year shall do better.' I shall never forget how beautifully mother answered him, though the dear, hopeful soul had built much on his success : but with a beaming face she kissed him, saying, ' I call that doing very well. Since you are safely home, dear, we don't ask anything else.' "

One of Miss Alcott's unfulfilled purposes was to write a story entitled " The Pathetic Family." This passage would have found a place in it. It deserves to be said that Mr. Alcott's faith that he had " opened a way and another year should do better," was justified. Fifteen years later, from one of his western tours, he brought home $700, but, thanks to Louisa's pen, the family were no longer in such desperate need of money.

More than once Miss Alcott declares that no one ever assisted her in her struggles, but that was far from true, as appears from many favors acknowledged in her journal. It was by the kindness of a lady who bought the manuscripts and assumed the risk of publication, that her first book, " Flower Fables," was brought out in 1854. It consisted of the fairy tales written six years before for the little Emersons. She received $32.00, a sum which would have seemed insignificant thirty years later when, in 1886, the sale of her books for six months brought her $8,000; but she says, " I was prouder over the $32.00 than over the $8,000."

The picture of Jo in a garret in " Little Women," planning and writing stories, is drawn from Louisa's experiences of the following winter. A frequent entry in her journal for this period is " $5.00 for a story " and her winter's earnings are summed up, " school, one quarter, $50, sewing $50, stories, $20." In December we read, " Got five dollars for a tale and twelve for sewing." Teaching, writing, and sewing alternate in her life for the next five years, and, for a year or two yet, the needle is mightier than the pen; but in 1856, she began to be paid $10 for a story, and, in 1859, the *Atlantic* accepted a story and paid her $50.

A friend for whose encouragement during these hard years, she acknowledges great indebtedness and who appears as one of the characters in her story, entitled " Work," was Rev. Theodore Parker, a man as helpful, loving,

and gentle as she depicts him, but then much
hated by those called orthodox and hardly in
good standing among his Unitarian brethren.
Miss Alcott, then as ever, had the courage of her
convictions, was a member of his Music Hall con-
gregation, and a regular attendant at his
Sunday evening receptions, finding him " very
friendly to the large, bashful girl who adorns
his parlor regularly." She " fought for him,"
she says, when some one said Mr. Parker " was
not a Christian. He is my sort; for though he
may lack reverence for other people's God, he
works bravely for his own, and turns his back on
no one who needs help, as some of the pious do."
After Mr. Parker's death, Miss Alcott, when in
Boston, attended the church of Dr. C. A. Bartol,
who buried her mother, her father and herself.

In 1857, the Alcotts returned to Concord,
buying and occupying the Orchard House,
which thenceforth became their home. Other
family events of the period were, the death of
Miss Alcott's sister Elizabeth, Beth in " Little
Women," the marriage of Anna, Meg in "Little
Women," and a proposal of marriage to Louisa,
serious enough for her to hold a consultation
over it with her mother. Miss Alcott is said to
have been averse to entangling alliances for her-

self, to have married off the heroines in her novels reluctantly at the demand of her readers, and never to have enjoyed writing the necessary love-passages.

The year 1860, when Miss Alcott is twenty-seven, has the distinction of being marked in the heading of her journal as " A Year of Good Luck." Her family had attained a comfortable, settled home in Concord; Mr. Alcott had been appointed superintendent of public schools, an office for which he was peculiarly well qualified and in which he was both happy and admirably successful; Anna, the eldest sister, was happily married; May, the youngest, was making a reputation as an artist; and Louisa, in perfect health, having in May before, " walked to Boston, twenty miles, in five hours, and attended an evening party," was becoming a regular contributor to the *Atlantic*, and receiving $50, $75, and sometimes $100 for her stories.

In these happy conditions, Miss Alcott sat down to a more ambitious attempt at authorship and wrote the first rough draft of " Moods," a " problem novel " that provoked much discussion and, though it caused her more trouble than any other of her books, was always dearest to her heart. It was written in a kind of frenzy of poetic enthusiasm. " Genius burned so fiercely," she says, " that for four weeks, I wrote all day and planned nearly all night, being quite possessed by my work. I was perfectly happy, and seemed to have no wants. Finished the book, or a rough draft of it, and put it away to settle." It was not published till four years later. Even in this year of good luck, there seem to have been some privations, as she records being invited to attend a John Brown meeting and declining because she " had no good gown." She sends a poem instead.

The breaking out of the Civil War stirred Miss Alcott's soul to its depths, and we have numerous references to its progress in her journal. " I like the stir in the air," she writes, " and long for battle like a war-horse when he smells powder." Not being permitted to enlist as a soldier, she went into a hospital in Washington as a nurse. Her experiences are graphically and dramatically told in " Hospital Sketches." That book, chiefly made from her private letters, met the demand of the public, eager for any information about the great war; it was widely read and, besides putting $200 in her purse, gave her a reputation with readers and publishers. Many applications for manuscript came in and she was told that " any publisher this side of Baltimore would be glad to get a book " from her. " There is a sudden hoist," she says, " for a meek and lowly scribbler. Fifteen years of hard grubbing may come to something yet." Her receipts for the year 1863, amounted to $600 and she takes comfort in saying that she had spent less than one hundred on herself.

The following year, after having been twice re-written, " Moods " was brought out and, thanks to the " Hospital Sketches," had a ready sale. Wherever she went, she says, she " found people laughing or crying over it, and was continually told how well it was going, how much it was liked, how fine a thing I had done." The first edition was exhausted in a week. An entire edition was ordered by London publishers. She was very well satisfied with the reception of " Moods " at the time, though in after years when fifty thousand copies of a book would be printed as a first edition, the sale of " Moods " seemed to her inconsiderable.

The present day reader wonders neither at the eagerness of the public for the book, nor at the criticisms that were freely made upon it. It is interesting from cover to cover and as a study

of " a life affected by moods, not a discussion
of marriage," it is effective. In spite, however,
of the warning of the author, everyone read it
as " a discussion of marriage," and few were
satisfied. The interest centres in the fortunes
of a girl who has married the wrong lover, the
man to whom, by preference, she would have
given her heart being supposed to be dead.
Would that he had been, for then, to all appearance, she would have been contented and
happy. Unfortunately he returns a year too
late, finds the girl married and, though endowed
with every virtue which a novelist can bestow
upon her hero, he does not know enough to leave
the poor woman in peace. On the contrary, he
settles down to a deliberate siege to find out how
she feels, wrings from her the confession that
she is miserable, as by that time no doubt she
was, and then convinces her that since she does
not love her husband, it is altogether wrong to
live under the same roof with him. Surely this
was nobly done. Poor Sylvia loves this villain,
Miss Alcott evidently loves him, but the bloody-
minded reader would like to thrust a knife into
him. However, he is not a name or a type, but a
real man, or one could not get so angry with
him. All the characters live and breathe in

these pages, and no criticism was less to the purpose than that the situations were unnatural. Miss Alcott says " The relations of Warwick, Moor, and Sylvia are pronounced impossible ; yet a case of the sort exists, and a woman came and asked me how I knew it. I did not know or guess, but perhaps felt it, without any other guide, and unconsciously put the thing into my book."

Everyone will agree that Miss Alcott had earned a vacation, and it came in 1865, in a trip to Europe, where she spent a year, from July to July, as the companion of an invalid lady, going abroad for health. The necessity of modulating her pace to the movements of a nervous invalid involved some discomforts for a person of Miss Alcott's pedestrian abilities, but who would not accept some discomforts for a year of European travel? She had a reading knowledge of German and French, and in the abundant leisure which the long rests of her invalid friend forced upon her, she learned to speak French with facility.

On her return from Europe, she found her circumstances much improved. She had established her position as a regular contributer to the *Atlantic* whose editor, she says, " takes all

I 'll send." In 1868, she was offered and accepted the editorship of *Merry's Museum* at a salary of $500, and, more important, she was asked by Roberts Brothers to " write a girl's book." Her response to this proposition was " Little Women," which she calls " the first golden egg of the ugly duckling, for the copyright made her fortune." Two editions were exhausted in six weeks and the book was translated into French, German and Dutch.

" Little Men " was written, a chapter a day, in November of the same year, and " An Old-fashioned Girl," a popular favorite, the year following. " Hospital Sketches " had not yet outlived its welcome, was republished, with some additions, in 1869, and two thousand copies were sold the first week. She is able to say, " Paid up all debts, thank the Lord, every penny that money can pay,— and now I feel as if I could die in peace." Besides, she has invested " $1,200 for a rainy day," and is annoyed because " people come and stare at the Alcotts. Reporters haunt the place to look at the authoress, who dodges into the woods."

The severe application which her achievement had cost had impaired Miss Alcott's fine constitution and, in 1870, taking May, her artist sister, she made a second trip to Europe, spending the summer in France and Switzerland and the winter in Rome. A charming account of the adventures of this expedition is given in "Shawl-Straps." A pleasant incident of the journey was the receipt of a statement from her publisher giving her credit for $6,212, and she is able to say that she has "$10,000 well invested and more coming in all the time," and that she thinks "we may venture to enjoy ourselves, after the hard times we have had."

In 1872, she published "Work: a story of Experience," and it is for the most part, a story of her own experience. "Christie's adventures," she says, "are many of them my own: Mr. Power is Mr. Parker: Mrs. Wilkins is imaginary, and all the rest. This was begun at eighteen, and never finished till H. W. Beecher wrote me for a serial **for** the *Christian Union* and paid $3,000 for it." It is one of the most deservedly popular of her books.

In 1877, for Roberts Brothers' "No Name Series," Miss Alcott wrote "A Modern Mephistopheles," her least agreeable book, but original, imaginative, and powerful. The moral of the story is that, in our modern life, the devil does not appear with a cloven foot, but as a cultivated man of the world. Miss Alcott's Mephistopheles is even capable of generous impulses. With the kindness of a Good Samaritan, he saves a poor wretch from suicide and then destroys him morally. The devil is apparently a mixed character with a decided preponderance of sinfulness.

Miss Alcott had now reached her forty-fifth year, had placed her family in independent circumstances, thus achieving her early ambition, and the effort began to tell upon her health. A succession of rapid changes soon came upon her. Mrs. Alcott, having attained her seventy-seventh year, was very comfortable for her age. " Mother is cosy with her sewing, letters, and the success of her ' girls,' " writes Miss Alcott in January; but in June, "Marmee grows more and more feeble," and in November the end came. " She fell asleep in my arms," writes Louisa; " My duty is done, and now I shall be glad to follow her."

May, the talented artist sister, whom Louisa had educated, had once taken to Europe and twice sent abroad for study, was married in London in 1878, to a Swiss gentleman of good family and some fortune, Mr. Nieriker. The marriage was a very happy one but the joy of the young wife was brief. She died the year following, leaving an infant daughter as a legacy to Louisa.

Mr. Emerson's death in 1882, was, to her, much like taking a member of her own family: " The nearest and dearest friend father ever had and the man who helped me most by his life, his books, his society. I can never tell all he has been to me,— from the time I sang Mignon's song under his window (a little girl) and wrote letters *a la Bettine* to him, my Goethe, at fifteen, up through my hard years, when his essays on Self-Reliance, Character, Compensation, Love, and Friendship helped me to understand myself and life, and God and Nature."

Mr. Alcott is still with her, vigorous for his years. In 1879, at the age of eighty, he inaugurated the Concord School of Philosophy, " with thirty students. Father the dean. He has his dream realized at last, and is in glory, with plenty of talk to swim in." The school was, for Miss Alcott, an expensive toy with which she was glad to be able to indulge her father. Personally she cared little for it. On one of her rare visits to it, she was asked her definition of a philosopher, and responded instantly: " My definition is of a man up in a balloon, with his family and friends holding the ropes which confine him to earth and trying to haul him down." For her father's sake, she rejoiced in the success of the enterprise. Of the second season, she writes, " The new craze flourishes. The first year, Concord people stood aloof; now the school is pronounced a success, because it brings money to the town. Father asked why we never went, and Anna showed him a long list of four hundred names of callers, and he said no more."

In addition to the labors which the school laid upon Mr. Alcott, he prepared for the press a volume of sonnets, some of which are excellent, especially one to Louisa:

" Ne'er from thyself by Fame's loud trump be-
    guiled,
Sounding in this and the farther hemisphere,—
I press thee to my heart as Duty's faithful
    child."

Mr. Alcott seemed to be renewing his youth but, in November, he was prostrated by paralysis. " Forty sonnets last winter," writes Louisa, " and fifty lectures at the school last summer, were too much for a man of eighty-three." He recovered sufficiently to enjoy his friends and his books and lingered six years, every want supplied by his devoted daughter.

With Miss Alcott the years go on at a slower pace, the writing of books alternating with sleepless nights and attacks of vertigo. " Jo's Boys " was written in 1884, fifty thousand copies being printed for the first edition. In 1886, her physician forbids her beginning anything that will need much thought. Life was closing in upon her, and she did not wish to live if she could not be of use. In March, 1888, Mr. Alcott failed rapidly, and died on the sixth of the month. Miss Alcott visited him and, in the excitement of leave-taking, neglected to wrap herself properly, took a fatal cold, and two days after, on the day of his burial, she followed him, in the fifty-sixth year of her age. Dr. C. A. Bartol, who had just buried her father, said tenderly at her funeral: " The two were so wont to be together, God saw they could not well live apart."

If Miss Alcott, by the pressure of circumstances, had not been a writer of children's books, she might have been a poet, and would, from choice, have been a philanthropist and reformer. Having worked her own way with much difficulty, it was impossible that she should not be

interested in lightening the burdens which lay
upon women, in the race of life, and though
never a prominent worker in the cause, she was
a zealous believer in the right of women to the
ballot. She attended the Woman's Congress in
Syracuse, in 1875, " drove about and drummed
up women to my suffrage meeting " in Concord,
she says, in 1879, and writes in a letter of 1881,
" I for one don't want to be ranked among idiots,
felons, and minors any longer, for I am none of
them."

To say that she might have been a poet does
her scant justice. She wrote two or three fine
lyrics which would justify giving her a high
place among the verse-writers of her generation.
" Thoreau's Flute," printed in the *Atlantic*, has
been called the most perfect of her poems, with
a possible exception of a tender tribute to her
mother. Personally, I consider the lines in
memory of her mother one of the finest elegiac
poems within my knowledge:

" Mysterious death: who in a single hour
     Life's gold can so refine,
     And by thy art divine,
Change mortal weakness to immortal power."

There are twelve stanzas of equal strength and

beauty. The closing lines of this fine eulogy we may apply to Miss Alcott, for both lives have the same lesson:

" Teaching us how to seek the highest goal,
     To earn the true success,—
     To live, to love, to bless,—
And make death proud to take a royal soul."